How could she go on?

Cindy was a prostitute and a drug addict. She had to give up her daughter to the Child Welfare Bureau because she could no longer take care of her. How could she go on alone with her life such a mess—and without her beloved little girl, Melody? Discover how Cindy freed herself from her miserable, degrading life of crime, sex, drugs and hopelessness. This moving story contains a powerful, positive message for all young people who are searching for happiness and meaning in a complex world.

CINDY

JOHN BENTON

SPIRE
BOOKS

Fleming H. Revell Company
Old Tappan, New Jersey

Library of Congress Cataloging in Publication Data

Benton, John, date
  Cindy.

  (Spire books)
  SUMMARY: Cindy's life of prostitution and her heroin
habit conflict with her responsibilities as a mother.
Can she be born again?
  [1. Prostitutes—Fiction. 2. Drug abuse—Fiction.
3. Christian life—Fiction] I. Title.
PZ4.B4788Ci [PS3552.E57] 813'.5'4 [Fic]   78-372
ISBN 0-8007-8319-0

This is an original Spire book, published by Spire Books, a Division
of Fleming H. Revell Company, Old Tappan, New Jersey

To Joyce Dyrud, who is a very special friend to Elsie and me. Besides being a very capable office manager and actress in our films, she's had a notably important part in my books and articles.

1

Cindy Lippincot squeezed farther under the bed. She listened breathlessly for the policemen's footsteps out in the hall.

A few moments before they had seen her on the street, copping drugs from Monty. But why had they chased *her* and not Monty? Every cop had the ultimate desire of busting a drug pusher. Instead they ran after her.

Maybe this was a crackdown on prostitutes. The cops were always burning a neighborhood by rounding up all the prostitutes.

It didn't matter now. Cindy could hear the pounding footsteps of the policemen getting closer to her door. If they caught her with the drugs . . . . She didn't even want to think about it. Her body ached to get off. But she had to hide. What rotten luck!

Cindy couldn't know it, but a newspaper was indirectly behind what was happening to her.

Early that morning in the business district Charles Seiburn arrived at his imposing office building. He didn't even wait for his chauffeur to open the door of his limousine. He was furious.

He had been reading the *New York Times* again. What aggravated him was another front-page article telling how various businesses were leaving for the suburbs. Always the reasons were the same: high crime rate, poor transportation, excessive taxes, enormous salaries. Unable to cope, many companies found their answer in the suburbs.

Not Charles Seiburn—he was determined that International Machine Company wouldn't join the exodus. New York City is where they had started sixty years ago; this is where they would stay.

Although New York did have its problems, he wanted to make his city the greatest in the world. *He* wouldn't move out; he would stay and fight!

He was so absorbed that he didn't respond when his driver, Tim, called out, "Have a good day, Mr. Seiburn." Tim tried again, "Have a good day, Mr. Seiburn." By this time he was almost to the front door. Tim waited for him to turn around, but he didn't. He slapped the *Times* against his thigh and disappeared inside.

Charles Seiburn strode into his office. Without even bothering to sit down, he punched the intercom button for his secretary.

"Lorraine, come here, please."

Lorraine grabbed her steno pad. She knew something was up.

Mr. Seiburn was staring at the traffic below. Without even turning around he started, "Lorraine, take a letter to Police Commissioner Paul Polzer.

"Dear Mr. Commissioner:

"In this morning's newspaper I read that more corporations are moving out of the city.

"I know the problems of our city are almost overwhelming, and I am sure you feel, as I do, that it is almost impossible to find out what's going wrong. However, I am one man who is determined to do something about it.

"One of the chief complaints is the high crime rate. What are you really doing about it? And please don't try to tell me that hiring more policemen will answer the problem. I expect something more intelligent than that.

"I expect to hear from you soon."

"Well," Lorraine responded when Mr. Seiburn turned around, "do you really think the police commissioner will do something?

"He'd better, or I'll get him fired. I'll go to see the mayor if I have to, and believe you me, the mayor would take care of him. I expect an answer!"

"I certainly agree about the high crime rate. But do you think this is the right approach?"

"I beg your pardon. What do you think is the answer?"

"I don't really know. And I'm not quite sure the police commissioner can solve the problem either."

Lorraine moved toward the door. "I'll have this letter for you in five minutes."

Lorraine's fingers began punching the keys of her typewriter. But about halfway through she stopped. She pushed the intercom.

"Mr. Seiburn, this is Lorraine. Would you mind if I came in a moment?"

"Of course not. Bring the letter with you."

"Uh . . . I'm not quite finished, but I'll be just a minute, and then I'll get it finished."

"What is it, Lorraine?" he asked as she entered.

"Mr. Seiburn, I just had an idea about your letter. This may sound kind of corny, but I heard somewhere that most of the crime here in the city is committed by drug addicts.''

"Come to think of it, Lorraine, I read that someplace too. But I don't care who is committing the crime; I just want it stopped. And the police commissioner had better do something about it!"

"Well, Mr. Seiburn, I'm sure a lot of people have gone to the commissioner, and it hasn't seemed to have helped. Maybe you can do something to help the drug addicts. Maybe if the addicts were really cured, they would stop committing crimes."

Charles Seiburn stroked his chin. "Hmmmm. Helping drug addicts. It would be good public relations for the company. And it would help the city. But how in the world could I help drug addicts? I don't know how to do that."

"Some organizations in our city are working with them," Lorraine responded. "I don't know much about it, but apparently someone is trying to do something."

Mr. Seiburn rubbed his chin again. Lorraine knew that meant he was seriously considering the idea. Could the answer to the crime in New York City really be found in helping to cure drug addicts?

"I'll tell you what, Lorraine. Let me do a little more research on this, and then I'll let you know what to do with that letter. Right now, get Glen on the phone. I'd like to see what he thinks about all this."

Glen Simmons was the major stockholder of the International Machine Company. Mr. Seiburn had a lot of confidence in his opinions. And he would certainly have to consult him about starting any major new program.

Just then Lorraine buzzed. "Mr. Simmons is on the line."

"Glen, I know you've been reading in the papers about the companies moving out of New York City. I'm just sick about it. I started to send a letter to Commissioner Polzer to do something to lower the crime rate here in the city, but my secretary had an idea. She suggested it would be better if our company did something to help cure drug addicts. What do you think?"

There was silence for a moment.

"Sounds like a pretty good idea, Charles. In fact my brother Kevin has this problem. His daughter has been on drugs for three years, and they have had enormous problems with her. If we could come up with something positive, it wouldn't hurt our company's image either. Why don't you pursue it and let me know? You have my blessings."

"Well, that's that," Mr. Seiburn said half aloud as he hung up. But where could he turn next? He knew nothing about drug problems or organizations working with addicts.

Maybe Lorraine knew. Secretaries always were a special help to presidents of corporations. It seemed as though a good secretary always had more practical information than the other officers. And Lorraine was a jewel!

Mr. Seiburn pushed the intercom again. Lorraine hurried into his office.

"Lorraine, Glen seems to think we should pursue this subject of helping the drug addicts."

"Great!"

"I suppose the first thing to do is to form a

committee—you know, something like a task force. Then we could relay our findings to the mayor.''

"A task force? Do you think that's the answer?"

"Well, we've solved other problems using this approach. Why not have a task force on drug addiction?" Mr. Seiburn began naming some of the employees who could serve, but somehow the idea didn't click. Besides, International Machine wasn't in the business of solving crime. His workers were good at making machinery, but this was certainly way out of their line.

"Maybe I got too irritated this morning, Lorraine. Maybe I should just simmer down and forget the whole thing."

"Oh, please don't do that, Mr. Seiburn. People are already afraid to go out alone. If the crime problem isn't solved, this city will become the worst place in the world to live. And if people don't want to live in New York, the days of International Machine Company are numbered. No, Mr. Seiburn, you *can't* give up. You've got a good idea, and I think we should pursue it. I'll do some research on it."

Lorraine went back to her desk. What could IMC do? How could they do it? Involuntarily she glanced at a stack of reports that had just been placed on her desk. Right there on top was one about Patti Amos. The name rang a bell. Amos . . . Amos . . . .

That was the name of an ex-drug addict IMC had hired about three years ago. Talk about coincidence. IMC was already helping an ex-drug addict! And maybe she would have some ideas about ways they could help others.

Lorraine buzzed her boss again. "I just ran across something, Mr. Seiburn. Several years ago we hired a girl who used to be a drug addict. She works down on the third floor in the foreign-business department. I have her work report here. She seems to be doing very well. Do you think she could help us?"

"Maybe that's the secret. I'd sure like to talk to an ex-drug addict to see what she has to say."

"I must tell you this, Mr. Seiburn. Her supervisor says she is quite religious. Do you mind that?"

Mr. Seiburn laughed. "Religion? Are you kidding? A little religion never hurt anybody!"

Lorraine hurriedly made arrangements. In a few minutes Patti walked into her office.

"Hello, there. I'm Lorraine Mullens, Mr. Seiburn's secretary. He is thinking about doing something to help drug addicts and would like to talk to you about the problems of crime and drug addiction. Do you mind?"

"Oh, no! I'd be glad to. But I'm kind of scared."

"Don't worry," Lorraine reassured her. "Mr. Seiburn may seem a little gruff now and then, but he doesn't bite."

Patti laughed nervously.

"Let me buzz him. I'm sure he's waiting for you."

Patti shifted her weight from one foot to the other and twisted her Kleenex. "Okay, Patti, we can go in now. Don't be afraid."

Lorraine introduced Patti, and Mr. Seiburn motioned to them to sit down.

"Patti, I understand you've been a drug addict," Mr. Seiburn began.

"Yes, sir, I was—for seven years."

"We have an enormous problem of crime in this city. I need some advice on dealing with this, and Lorraine suggested I talk to you about how crime and drug addiction are related. Could you tell me a little about your background?''

"My start in life wasn't like the usual baby's ," Patti said. "I was born addicted to heroin. You see, my mother and father both were heroin addicts. With my mother having a habit, I was born addicted. Of course I don't remember, but my mother did tell me I had withdrawal from heroin as a baby. I guess it's one of the most horrible things anybody could see. But, thank God, I made it through."

Charles Seiburn frowned. "I just can't imagine a person getting a start in life like that—a drug addict from the first breath they took. Then what happened?"

"I really don't remember much about when I was little. I grew up in the jungles of Washington, D.C., in a dog-eat-dog world. Everyone was out for himself.

"I remember my mother and father always talked about money. Not only were they addicts—they were pushers too. They bragged about how much money they made pushing. But selling drugs only increased their own personal drug habits. It was an endless cycle with no way out.

"Then when I was ten, they were both jailed for possession of narcotics."

"What happened to you?" Mr. Seiburn asked.

"That's part of my life I will never forget. It was in the evening, and I was home alone. My parents told me never to answer the door. So when I heard this knock, of course I didn't answer it.

"Then someone shouted, 'Open up! This is the police!' I was terrified and went and hid behind the couch. They shouted again. I hardly dared breathe.

"All of a sudden I heard this loud bang, and they crashed the door down. I tried to slide under the couch. But in a few minutes a policeman pushed back the couch and pulled me out.

"They took me down to the precinct. Because it was so late, they had to put me in youth detention. That was my first time in jail."

"Just ten years old and in jail? How tragic!" Mr. Seiburn obviously was moved.

"I can still remember sitting there in jail and becoming bitter," Patti continued. "I was really mad at the world because my parents weren't like regular parents, and I really couldn't have a mother to come home to. My mother was a drug addict, and, besides that, I knew she had to go out and be a prostitute to support her habit.

"My father wasn't a regular father. He was a drug pusher. Some of the kids knew this, and they really teased me. Then I had to sit in that jail cell when I was just ten years old. I was really mad at the world. I didn't ask to be born a drug addict. I didn't ask for my parents. I didn't ask to go to jail. Then and there I determined I was going to get even with my parents and get back at the world.

"The next day they sent me to a foster home. I was there six months, and then they sent me to another. The first parents said I was incorrigible and was wrecking their family. To tell you the truth, that family didn't have any patience with me. I think they just took me to get the monthly check from welfare. Well, anyway, I went to another family for two years."

"I assume you did go to school," Mr. Seiburn interrupted.

"Yes, I went to school, but I didn't get very good grades. Then when my parents were released, I was able to go back with them."

Mr. Seiburn smiled. "I assume they had learned their lesson and changed their ways?"

"No. As usual, it wasn't long before my father was selling drugs and my mother was out on the streets again. I stayed with them two or three more years, and I ran away. I was sixteen.

"I ended up on the streets of New York, and a pimp took me in. He drove a real fancy car, and I stayed in his plush apartment. What I didn't know was that he was setting me up. It wasn't long until he had me out in the streets, selling me, and he was making all the profits."

"You mean you came here to this city as a sixteen-year-old runaway, and you were out on the streets as a prostitute at that age?" Mr. Seiburn looked at her unbelievingly.

"Yes, sir. In fact there are many teenage girls in the city now who are prostitutes. Poor things, they're afraid to go home because there's not really a home to go to. And they're afraid to stay in the city because of the problems of being a prostitute. They can't run to the cops and squeal on their pimps because the pimps would probably kill them. They are really in a bind. I feel so sorry for them."

Mr. Seiburn looked over at Lorraine. Were they both thinking the same thing? "This city has turned into a haven for runaways, but it's no good for them. Maybe the problem is in prostitution," Lorraine suggested.

"Maybe I'm taking too long telling you what happened," Patti interjected. "Do you still want me to go on?"

"Of course. I understand you are one of our best secretaries, and I really want to find out how you ended up here. You certainly don't look as if you're on drugs now. Are you?"

Patti chuckled. "No, of course not. And that's the good part I want to tell you about in just a moment. But first let me give you a couple more examples of what happened to me."

Mr. Seiburn and Lorraine nodded approval and leaned forward in their chairs.

"Well, out there in the street doing the things I knew weren't right, I had to find some peace of mind. So I turned to drugs. I felt so very guilty about what I was doing and what had happened to me and all that bitterness and those kinds of things, but it just seemed that whenever I took drugs, I got high, and peace came over me. But that peace didn't last very long, and I doubted if there would ever be a way out.

"Then one evening I got busted by an undercover cop. I was taken to jail and had to detoxify. I was sentenced to thirty days.

"And then a most wonderful thing happened to me. While I was in jail, a Mrs. Benton came to see me. She was from the Walter Hoving Home. That's a home for girls like me upstate in Garrison, New York. She explained to me that Jesus wanted to change my life around and set me free from my drug addiction. When I first talked to her, I thought she was crazy. But she seemed to be such a kind person that I wanted to listen to what she had said."

"You mean, while you were in jail this Mrs. Benton

came to see you?" Mr. Seiburn asked. "Didn't your mother and father ever contact you?"

"No, sad to say. My parents weren't really interested in me. In fact once when I was out in the streets, I called home and talked to both of them. But they were too busy to bother. I guess they had written me off."

Lorraine looked startled. "You mean to tell me that your parents really didn't want anything more to do with you?"

"No, they didn't," Patti responded. "And I know that's sad. But I had some even sadder news not long after I had been arrested. Both my parents died of overdoses."

Patti bowed her head. There was a long pause.

"I'm very sorry to hear that, Patti," Mr. Seiburn said consolingly. "I'm sure that was quite a blow to you."

"Well, I was still bitter then. But I guess there is something about the death of your mother and father that affects you even when you are bitter. I knew it was good-bye forever. It was rather hard . . . .

"But let me go on. The following week Mrs. Benton came back and gave me a book to read. It was called *Carmen.* Her husband, director of the Walter Hoving Home, had written it."

"Say, I've heard about that book," Lorraine interrupted. "In fact I saw it on the newsstand."

"Yes, I understand it has sold very well," Patti said.

"Lorraine, make a note to get me a copy," Mr. Seiburn said. "Maybe we should get in touch with this organization. What's the book about?"

"It's a novel," Patti answered, "and it's about a girl

addict. Yet everything that happened to Carmen has happened to the girls at the Home.

"It was such an interesting book that when I got through reading it, I decided to call the Walter Hoving Home and see if they could help me. It was one of the most amazing stories I had ever read. I felt that if Carmen could get help, I could too.

"As soon as I called, Mrs. Benton—they call her Mom B at the Home—came back to jail and talked to me some more. In that jail cell I received Jesus as my personal Saviour."

"You did what?" Mr. Seiburn asked.

"I received Jesus as my Saviour. You know, asking Jesus to come into your heart?"

"That's interesting," Mr. Seiburn responded. "Is that what some people call being born again? I've heard that term a lot lately."

A great big smile crossed Patti's face. "Yes, sir. It's just like starting life all over again. And that's possible because Jesus lives right in my heart. No matter where I go, He's always with me."

"That sounds rather simplistic, Patti," Lorraine interrupted. "But go on."

"Mom B was able to talk to the probation department, and the judge gave me a break and sent me to the Walter Hoving Home. I went there and graduated from the Home a couple of years ago. While I was there, I learned to apply God's Word to my life and everyday circumstances, and I also had the privilege of telling other girls what Jesus could do for them. In fact I've sent a number of girls up to the Home from the city. They were drug addicts, and believe you me, Christ is doing the same thing for them that He has done for me.

Real miracles are happening.''

Mr. Seiburn leaned back in his overstuffed chair. He really couldn't believe what he was hearing. How could this beautiful little girl who was such a good secretary be born a drug addict, be neglected as a child, live a drug addict's life, and yet have such a complete turnaround? He had never heard of anything like this before.

''Mr. Seiburn,'' Patti continued, ''do you know what the most wonderful part of the story is?''

''No, what is it?''

Patti leaned forward. All signs of nervousness were gone. She pointed her finger at Mr. Seiburn. ''What Jesus has done for me, He wants to do for you!''

''What? I'm no drug addict!''

Patti chuckled. ''I know that, Mr. Seiburn. From working here I've heard you are a wonderful man and run a very good business. But there is something missing in all our lives until Jesus comes in and makes us complete.''

Mr. Seiburn squirmed and then stood up. ''Patti, I am very happy for you. I think it's just absolutely beautiful and wonderful what's happened to you. But it's not for me.''

Patti stood too. ''I know how you feel, Mr. Seiburn. I used to feel the same way—that Jesus was for other people, not for me. But one day I suddenly realized that He really *was* for me, and that's what's made all the difference in my life. I'm so glad I took Him as my Saviour. I hope you do too. I can just see how God could use you in such a special way if you were a Christian and president of this tremendous business.''

Mr. Seiburn hadn't expected that kind of response.

The very idea of God using him seemed rather far-fetched. He respected God, but . . . .

Lorraine broke the awkward pause. "Patti, I think you'd better go back down to your desk. Mr. Seiburn has another appointment in a few minutes."

After Patti left, Mr. Seiburn asked Lorraine to stay for a few minutes to discuss what they had just witnessed.

"What do you think of that, Lorraine?" he started. "Do you think she made all that up? After all, drugs can affect a person's mind."

"I warned you she was very religious," Lorraine answered. "But I think she is sincere. I can't doubt her experience. I had heard a little about it before."

Mr. Seiburn asked, "Do you think we can trust her? After all, she *is* a former addict. Sometimes those people revert to their old problems."

"I thought about that too, Mr. Seiburn. But I talked to her supervisor before I called her. Patti has one of the best work records of any of our secretaries. She is always on time for work, puts in her very best, and gets along with everyone. In fact they claim she's a ray of sunshine in that area."

"I just don't know what to think, Lorraine. She mentioned a home working with drug addicts. Maybe I could check that out with the police commissioner."

Just then the phone rang. Lorraine answered it. "Just a minute. Mr. Simmons. He's right here."

"Charles, I hope you're really getting into that drug-addict thing."

"Well, Glen, we were just talking . . . ."

"Look, a friend of my mother's was just mugged over on Forty-second Street—by a girl! I'm sure she was an addict—probably a prostitute too. Most of them are. Mother wanted to know if I could get something done."

"I think Lorraine has that letter ready, Glen. I'll get it off to Commissioner Polzer right away."

"We don't have a week for a letter to get across town. Go on down there and see him. Let's get some action *today*."

"Right, Glen. I'll see what I can do. Something's got to be done."

2

Lorraine was back at her desk when Mr. Seiburn buzzed again. "Call the police commissioner's office and see if he is in."

Lorraine dialed City Hall. The police commissioner was in.

"I didn't tell them who was calling," Lorraine reported, "so they wouldn't pull any fast ones and try to escape or something. I think you should drop in unannounced and tell him what the problem is."

"I've been thinking about what the problem really is. From what Patti said, it seems to me that one of the great problems of the city is prostitution. Apparently some of these girls become drug addicts. If we got all the prostitutes off the streets, that would certainly help solve the problem, wouldn't it?"

"Yes, that really would solve a big problem, Mr. Seiburn. I never could understand why the police didn't just go out and round up all the prostitutes and put them in jail. Then if we filled up all the jails . . ." Lorraine paused. "If we filled the jails, then we could send for this Mrs. Benton Patti was talking about. She could save all these girls and really solve our problems!" Lorraine chuckled at her own cleverness.

But Mr. Seiburn didn't laugh. "These prostitutes are bringing in all sorts of crime, Lorraine. And the police don't seem to be doing a thing about it. Why, I wouldn't be surprised if some of them are on the take.

I'll bet that commissioner hasn't even tried to touch the problem."

Mr. Seiburn obviously was agitated again—just as he had been when he arrived this morning. Lorraine decided it would be best to return to her desk.

Charles Seiburn grabbed his briefcase. "Call Tim and have him meet me at the front door. I hope I won't be long."

He could see it clearly now. The first step was to get those girls off the streets. He wondered what kind of reception he would get at the police commissioner's office. *The commissioner had better do something,* he told himself, *or I will take matters into my own hands.*

Tim was waiting with the door open when Mr. Seiburn stepped out of the office building. Tim had been his chauffeur for fifteen years. Never once had he been late. It seemed almost that he lived in the car and responded quickly—like a fireman.

It didn't take a psychologist to see that Mr. Seiburn was still upset.

"Where to, sir?"

"Drive over to Forty-second Street and turn on Eighth Avenue."

"Yes, sir."

Forty-second and Eighth Avenue? What was over there that would interest Mr. Seiburn? That's where all the peep shows, pornography shops, pimps, drug addicts, and prostitutes hung out. What would Mr. Seiburn be doing over there?

As they arrived at Forty-second Street, Tim turned right onto the one-way street. He drove a couple of blocks and glanced back.

Mr. Seiburn opened his briefcase.

That was strange. Mr. Seiburn rarely opened his briefcase in the car. Tim glanced ahead at the traffic.

When they stopped for a traffic light, Tim again glanced in the rearview mirror. Mr. Seiburn was making notes on a yellow legal pad. When Mr. Seiburn glanced to the left, Tim looked over that way too. He saw two prostitutes on the corner.

The light changed, and he took off. But he kept looking in the mirror whenever he could. When Mr. Seiburn glanced to the right, Tim glanced to the right. Again it was the same thing—more prostitutes.

Tim began to worry. Certainly Mr. Seiburn wasn't looking for one of those girls, was he?

"Slow down," Mr. Seiburn ordered.

Tim slowed and waited for the order to stop. But nothing was said.

Tim glanced back again. He saw Mr. Seiburn look out the window and write something on his legal pad. What was he up to?

Being a chauffeur for fifteen years, Tim had heard some strange things from the president of the corporation. He had heard about the shenanigans of visiting salesmen. Tim knew Mr. Seiburn wasn't that type. He was happily married and had wonderful children.

Tim's curiosity was rising. Maybe if he added some humor to it, Mr. Seiburn wouldn't object to a question.

"Uh, Mr. Seiburn, those certainly are good-looking chicks out there, aren't they?"

Mr. Seiburn didn't say a word.

"If you want me to, I'll bet I can get you a date with a couple of them. Do you like blondes, redheads, or those with wigs?"

Still no comment.

Tim decided to try another tactic. "I'll bet those

girls would make good secretaries, don't you think?''

"Please, Tim. I'm doing some research. Just drive ahead without any comment.''

So that was it! Tim had heard before about these so-called research projects. They were just a front. These people would walk into pornography shops under the guise of doing research. Or they would go to X-rated movies. That "research" was a bunch of baloney. These guys just had a dirty desire to see what was going on. Certainly Mr. Seiburn wasn't one of those, was he?

Tim again glanced back. Mr. Seiburn was seething. He put his pad back into his briefcase. "All right, Tim. Let's go down to City Hall. I want to see the police commissioner. I'm going to get him to do something to get these girls off the streets.''

Tim breathed a sigh of relief.

When they stopped at City Hall, Mr. Seiburn said, "I shouldn't be over fifteen or twenty minutes. Wait here.''

Tim nodded.

Once inside, Charles Seiburn asked directions to the commissioner's office. Without looking up, the officer at the desk pointed down the hall. There it was on a large sign: PAUL POLZER, POLICE COMMISSIONER.

Mr. Seiburn walked in and gave his card to the secretary. Asking him to be seated a moment, she disappeared into the inner office. But Charles Seiburn was too upset by what he had seen. He couldn't sit down.

"Charles Seiburn, president and chairman of the board of International Machine Company, is here to see you, Commissioner.''

"That's just great. And what does *he* want?"

"He didn't say, but he's obviously upset. I mean, you know, you can tell by the way they look. And he looked like he was out for blood. Know what I mean?"

"You better believe I know. These big-shot businessmen are all alike. They're always giving me a bad time and trying to tell me what to do. They all think they know more about the job than I do. I'd like to get these birds out at 2:00 A.M. up in Harlem. Then they'd know what it's all about!"

Commissioner Polzer was obviously pleased with his analysis of the situation. "Send him in."

Charles Seiburn was still pacing when the secretary returned. "Commissioner Polzer would be delighted to see you, Mr. Seiburn," she announced.

Delighted! That's news! Maybe the commissioner really will be cooperative, he thought as he was ushered into the inner office.

The commissioner arose and extended his hand. "Mr. Seiburn, I'm delighted to meet you. I've heard a lot about you and your fine company. What can I do for you?"

"Commissioner Polzer, I'll get right to the point. Our city is being overrun with prostitutes. Many of them are drug addicts . . . ."

The commissioner had heard that one before. In fact just last year an ambassador to the United Nations had been propositioned by a prostitute. He said no, and the prostitute killed him. Federal agents had really put the pressure on after that one.

"All the businessmen in my association are fed up with this situation. What are you going to do about it?" Mr. Seiburn's voice was rising.

"I'm very much aware of the problem, Mr. Seiburn," Commissioner Polzer replied. "In fact our vice squad is always out on the streets doing its very best. This is only one of the many problems our department deals with every day. And, as you know, we're understaffed . . . ."

Mr. Seiburn abruptly sat down and opened his briefcase. He jerked out the yellow pad.

"I've just ridden along Eighth Avenue. And from Forty-second Street to Fifty-second Street I personally counted thirty-two streetwalkers and one lone policeman. Is that what you call dealing with the problem?"

Commissioner Polzer bristled.

"What do you want me to do—lock all those girls up? We don't have enough jails in this city to put them all in. Mr. Seiburn, as far as I'm concerned, it's a lost cause!"

"Well, that's exactly why I'm here," Mr. Seiburn shouted. "We've got to do something about this problem. If you think it's a lost cause, then I'll personally take it upon myself to make sure something is done! Do you understand what I mean?"

"For crying out loud, Seiburn, do you want me to go out there and shoot them all?"

Charles Seiburn realized that his anger wasn't helping. "Now, Commissioner, don't get me wrong. I know there are no easy answers. My purpose in coming to you is to do something practical to solve the problem."

Commissioner Polzer calmed too. "Mr. Seiburn, I give you my word, I'll do what I can."

"Commissioner, I have a question that's on my mind."

"Only one?"

"Do you really care about all those girls out there who are selling their bodies to support drug habits?"

Mr. Seiburn waited. Commissioner Polzer stared at him and then down at his desk. There was deadly silence.

Commissioner Polzer stuck out his hand. "Thank you for coming, Mr. Seiburn. I will try to do my best."

Well, that seemed easy. But would Commissioner Polzer really go out and clean up the streets? Many well-meaning people had tried before, but they always failed. Would the police department finally take action?

3

Commissioner Paul Polzer couldn't concentrate on anything else after Charles Seiburn had left his office. He sensed that something would have to be done immediately or the executive would take matters into his own hands.

He grabbed his hat and walked out. "Bonnie," he said to his secretary, "I'm going down to the Thirty-fourth Precinct. I'll be gone a couple of hours. If someone needs me, buzz Captain Heartley. And tell Delgado to bring my car around."

"What's bothering you?" Officer Delgado asked when the commissioner arrived at his car. "You look like you just had a fight with your wife."

"No, not quite. It's one of those businessmen on my back again. This time it's Seiburn, president of International Machine. He's been out counting prostitutes. I don't think he knows it, but I'm really getting a lot of heat from the business community about these prostitutes and drug addicts. Something's got to be done. We've got to clean up this mess."

"But can we do it?" Delgado asked.

"You'd better believe it. We're going to arrest every hooker and junkie on the streets. We'll bust their heads until not one of them will dare walk the streets of New York. When I'm finished, every businessman in this city will be proud of the job I've done."

In a few minutes they pulled up in front of the Thirty-fourth Precinct, and both walked inside. Uniformed policemen and detectives jumped to attention. They knew Commissioner Polzer.

The commissioner stopped at the front desk. "Sergeant Guinan, I want to talk to the men of this precinct. I need some help."

"We're just changing shifts now, and this is a good time," Guinan answered. "I'll get them in, sir, and we'll meet in the squad room."

A few minutes later the commissioner stood to address the gathered policemen.

"Gentlemen, I've got a problem. One of the most influential men in the city came to my office today to discuss the problem of prostitutes on our streets. They are overrunning this city like rats and roaches, and I've got to do something about it. Now, I'll need your full cooperation. Understand?"

A number of them nodded. As far as they were concerned, whatever the commissioner wanted, he got.

"Here's my problem," the commissioner continued. "I just had a visit from a Mr. Charles Seiburn, president of International Machine Company. He's hot under the collar about these prostitutes on the streets. And just yesterday I got a call from the mayor. I guess he's been getting some complaints too. He chewed me out, so the heat is really on me. My job is on the line. If that's the case, a lot of heads right in this room will roll with mine if we don't clean up this mess. Understand?"

More of the officers nodded. Cutbacks on the police force were the "in" thing. None of them wanted to lose their jobs.

Commissioner Polzer was shouting now. "This has got to stop. I think I have heard from every businessman in the city. The only one I haven't heard from is the sanitation commissioner."

Several officers laughed.

"That's not funny!" The commissioner was getting redder.

"This is what we're going to do. I want all you men to get out in the streets and start rounding up these girls. I'll be out there with Delgado, and I'll be busting girls left and right. Does everybody understand what I'm saying?"

They were all nodding now. They weren't about to mess around with a mad police commissioner!

"Okay, that's it. Let's all move out!"

The officers quickly exited. Commissioner Polzer and Delgado were back to their car in record time.

"Okay, Delgado, let's drive on up to Eighth Avenue. We'll cover the beat from Forty-second Street to Fifty-second Street. Seiburn said he saw thirty-two prostitutes there."

"Lovely neighborhood," Delgado responded sarcastically.

The commissioner ignored the comment. "So help me, Delgado, if I see the mayor's daughter out in the street and up to no good, I'll bust her too."

Delgado laughed. "Yeah, she is kinda cute."

Commissioner Polzer was still mad. "I'll show those guys in City Hall what's going on."

When they got to Eighth Avenue and Forty-second Street, Delgado slowed down.

"Delgado, look over there!" Commissioner Polzer said. "Is that girl copping drugs?"

"You better believe it! That pusher just handed her something!"

"Let's get them!"

Delgado pulled alongside. Spotting the patrol car, the boy started to run one way, and the girl ran straight ahead. It was Cindy—in trouble again.

Cindy wasn't new at this business. She'd been an addict for five years. She had just "copped" a bag from Monty. She needed a fix and wasn't about to get busted. Jail was no place for her!

Trying to ignore the siren, Cindy turned right at the corner. It wasn't far to her apartment now. As she burst into the tenement-house door and pounded up the stairs, she could hear the police car screeching to a halt. They had seen her come in and would be right behind her.

Oh, no! Cindy thought. *I can't get caught again!*

When she hit the second floor, she ran to the end of the hallway, threw open the window, then ran back about ten feet and squeezed into her apartment. She quietly locked the door and crawled under her unmade bed. With a sigh of relief she said to herself, *I made it!*

But had she? Footsteps pounded up the stairs, and down the hall. Then they stopped. She heard one of the men ask, "Which one do you think she's in?"

"Only one way to find out," Delgado said.

He took his billy club and rapped on a door. A woman opened the door slightly, eyeing the two policemen suspiciously.

"Yeah?" the woman said.

"Did a girl just run in here?"

"Girl? I ain't seen no girl." She slammed the door.

"Try the next door," Commissioner Polzer ordered.

Officer Delgado pounded on the next door. There was no answer. He pounded again—still no answer.

He moved on to the next door and pounded—no answer.

"She's got to be in one of them. Why don't we bust the door down, Commissioner?"

"Sure," the commissioner answered sarcastically. "I can see the papers now. 'Commissioner Polzer and his thugs break down doors of innocent people looking for lone little girl.' "

"Yeah, I guess you're right. But I know how we can tell which apartment she's in."

"How's that?"

"It's a trick I learned from Detective Moak."

Delgado walked down the hallway feeling each doorknob.

"What are you doing?"

"Just a minute. I'm not quite through."

Delgado wiped his hand on his shirt and went to the next door. Again he felt the doorknob.

"Come on, Delgado. What in the world are you doing? You're not a mystic or something like that, are you?"

"Naw. I'm checking for warmth and moisture. You see, her hands were probably hot and sweaty from being chased."

"Very clever!"

"Not so clever. They all feel the same."

"Hey," Commissioner Polzer said. "Look at that open window. I'll bet she went out there and down the fire escape!"

They ran to the window and looked down. The back lot was typical tenement: garbage strewn all over, overgrown with weeds. And no one was in sight.

"Think she went out the window?"

"Maybe," Delgado replied. "But I just remembered. Detective Moak also taught me about what people do to deploy. He said they would even open a window but then go in another direction. I still think she's in one of these three apartments. Let's give them another try."

Delgado walked up to the apartment door closest to the window. "I have a sneaking suspicion she's in here." He rapped on the door with his billy club.

Cindy slipped further under the bed. Would they bust the door down and haul her off to jail? She hid her face in her hands and hoped for the best.

Delgado rapped again. "Open up in there," he yelled. "This is the police."

Cindy held her breath. It seemed like an eternity.

"I still think we should bust the door down," Delgado said. "If she's in there, she's got drugs on her, and we'll have our first arrest."

Cindy knew what it meant if they caught her with drugs. She'd be off to prison again. Not only was going to jail one of the worst things in life, but to kick the habit while in jail was the greatest agony she had ever endured.

Cindy waited. It was agonizing.

"Come on, Delgado, Let's go. There are more girls out there on the street."

"I still think she's in there."

"Like I say," the commissioner replied, "there are plenty of girls out there. Remember, Seiburn counted thirty-two. Don't worry; we'll grab another."

Cindy could hear their footsteps fading in the distance. Maybe it was a trick. She waited but heard nothing.

Breathing a great sigh of relief, she crawled out from under the bed. Maybe now she could get off.

She looked around. Her apartment certainly wasn't the best. Dirty clothes were strewn about. Dishes, unwashed for several days, filled the sink. The garbage can was full, and the stench was gagging.

But what can you expect when you're a junkie? Being on drugs is a time-consuming job: twenty-four hours a day, seven days a week; no vacation; and certainly no retirement plan. Drugs were your master; you were their slave.

Sure the officers were really gone, Cindy headed toward her bathroom. Behind the toilet bowl she kept her works. She reached in and grabbed her needle, bottle cap, and matches. She quickly got her cooker going and got off. She felt the flash. Peace like a river began to flow through her mind. *This is where it's at,* she thought.

Cindy put the works away and walked to her bed. She sat on the edge of it and began to nod.

About an hour later she decided to go down to the corner coffeeshop for her usual coffee. But this just wasn't her day. She hadn't half finished her coffee when two pimps pulled up outside. Jimmy and Ben were looking for Cindy. She worked for them; rather, she was *supposed* to be working for them. They knew that if Cindy wasn't on the streets, she was usually at the coffeeshop.

Jimmy and Ben got out of the pimpmobile, walked to the door, and glanced in. Sure enough, there was Cindy, slumped over, sipping her coffee. They knew what had happened. Cindy had just gotten off.

Ben and Jimmy wondered how much she had been

making on the street. She usually brought three
hundred to five hundred dollars a night. She knew
where it was at and made good money for them. But
now they were having trouble with her. She wasn't as
willing as she used to be.

Jimmy swaggered up. "Made enough to retire,
Cindy?"

Cindy slowly turned around. She tried to focus her
eyes. As she realized who it was she jerked her head
back. "Uh, Jimmy, I just can't do it anymore. I'm
tired of this life. Come on. Give me a break!"

Ben stepped forward and grabbed her blouse near
the shoulder. Pulling her up close to his face, he said,
"Hey, Baby, this ain't no time to quit. The streets are
loaded with 'johns,' and you've got plenty of tricks
left."

Ben looked over at Jimmy and grinned. "Yeah, and
don't forget about that monkey on your back!"

Cindy knew all about the monkey on her back. She
wanted out. "I told you, I'm through! I'm giving it up!
I don't want to work for you anymore!"

Jimmy turned and nodded to Ben. Ben grabbed
Cindy and lifted her off her chair. Jimmy grabbed the
other side and jerked her off the floor. They started out
with her between them.

Ben turned toward the cashier. He reached into his
pocket and with a flourish pulled out a dollar bill and
threw it down with a grin. "For the coffee, my man."

The cashier didn't say a word. He knew the pimps.
They were mean. No sense messing with them. As it
was, he got a dollar. If he interfered, he'd get a cut-up
face.

The three headed toward the pimpmobile. Cindy's

befuddled brain was beginning to size up what was happening. She struggled. It was no use. Ben and Jimmy only tightened their grips.

Jimmy opened the door. Ben threw Cindy in with, "Nobody quits us, Baby."

Ben climbed into the back and put his arm around Cindy. He wasn't making love. "If you yell, I'll jam my fist down your throat," he threatened.

Cindy knew enough to keep quiet. She was hoping for the best but expecting the worst. She knew about other girls who didn't obey their pimps. Some were still around. But they were a sad sight with their broken arms or broken legs and their beaten-up faces.

Jimmy drove down to the lower East Side. He pulled into a vacant street where burned-out tenements stood like blackened tombstones. Nobody was around.

"Okay, Jimmy, do your stuff," Ben ordered.

Jimmy jumped out and jerked Cindy after him. He grabbed her arm and turned it up her back, pushing upwards. The pain in her shoulders and elbow was excruciating.

"What are you going to do to me?" Cindy cried.

"You know better than to ask questions. You know what you're supposed to do, and you haven't done it. And now you're going to pay—one way or the other."

Jimmy dragged Cindy around to the back side of the vacant tenement building, pushed her up against the wall, and began to slap her. Then he kicked.

Cindy fought back, and Jimmy hit her some more. He turned to yell to Ben for help. Cindy saw her chance and made a break for it.

She hadn't run more than ten feet when Jimmy tackled her. He flipped her over and began beating her face. Cindy reached up for his eyes. With her long fingernails she raked his face, and the blood flowed.

Jimmy screamed, clenched his fist, and belted Cindy in the mouth. Cindy kicked again. Jimmy rolled over, screaming in pain.

Jumping up, Cindy headed for the street. She had just turned the corner, and there stood Ben. He grabbed her and started to slap her. Cindy screamed.

Another car had entered the street. The driver slowed. Ben loosened his grip just long enough for Cindy to wrench free and run. Ben glared at the driver, who then quickly drove off.

Cindy was still running. There was a subway entrance! Her first bit of good luck all day! She ran down the steps and stood against the wall and waited. There was no sound.

A couple of people passed by and glanced at her but didn't offer to help.

If she could get on the subway, she could get back to her apartment. But how could she? She had no money.

A man was just starting by. "Hey, mister," she yelled. "You got fifty cents for a subway token? I was just walking down the steps here, and some guy jumped me and beat me up and snatched my purse. Could you please help me?"

The man eyed her suspiciously. "You're in bad shape, lady. You look more like a truck ran over you. Are you sure you're all right?"

"Yeah, I'm all right. If you'll just give me fifty cents for the subway, I'll go to the hospital, and they'll fix me up. Okay?"

The man reached in his pocket and pulled out two quarters.

"Thanks," Cindy called as she hurried over to get her subway token.

As she got on the subway, her pain was excruciating. Her face began to swell. She reached up and wiped the blood off her mouth once again. And she realized she had been lucky!

When she got off at her stop, her legs ached so badly that she could hardly get up the steps. She staggered the two blocks to her tenement. As she struggled up the stairs, she thought she heard something. Had the police come back? Or were Jimmy and Ben waiting in her apartment? Maybe her mind was playing tricks on her.

She stopped to rest a moment before starting down the hall to her apartment. By leaning against the wall she was able to make it to the door. She fumbled with the handle and then dragged herself inside.

The cold water she splashed on her face helped a little. Then someone knocked at the door. *Oh, no!* Cindy thought. *Not again!*

"Cindy? Is that you in there? Open up. It's Mrs. Johnson from across the hall. I need to talk to you."

Cindy opened the door a crack. Mrs. Johnson gasped. "What ever happened to you? Where have you been?"

"Oh, just out," Cindy said, ignoring the first question.

Just then Cindy's little girl, Melody, ran from behind Mrs. Johnson and pushed open the door, shouting, "Mommy! Mommy!"

Cindy threw her arms around Melody. They loved each other so much. But, of course, Melody was much too young to understand what was happening.

"Cindy, I . . . I . . . . Well, I don't think I can keep this up . . ." Mrs. Johnson started.

"It won't be much longer now, Mrs. Johnson, I'm expecting some money any day now."

"Cindy, it's not just the money. There is a problem . . . with you being out all the time, and the social workers . . . . By the way, that one was here again today from the Bureau of Child Welfare to check on Melody. If you ask me, you're going to have her taken away from you."

Cindy became quite belligerent. "Don't say that. No one is ever going to take Melody away from me. She'll never end up in an institution!"

"Well, I'm not going to be involved in this anymore," Mrs. Johnson snapped back with finality. "Find somebody else to take care of your kid." She turned abruptly and slammed the door.

Cindy was still hugging Melody. "You're all I've got, Baby. You're going to stay with me!"

Cindy moved over by the window and stared. Was there no way out? It was one thing after another: the police, the pimps, the beating, the drugs. Now the social worker . . . . She stood there for about ten minutes, just staring.

"Here, Mommy. Here's your medicine."

Melody's voice brought her out of her trance. There Melody stood, arms outstretched. In her hands was the hypodermic needle.

"Where did you get that?" Cindy screamed.

"Behind the toilet." Melody looked as if she couldn't understand what she had done wrong.

Cindy grabbed the needle. Abruptly she walked over

and opened the top dresser drawer. Melody couldn't reach it in there. She pushed back some unpressed blouses. There was her gun. Cindy turned to see if Melody was watching. Good—now Melody was staring out the window.

Cindy pushed the gun aside and laid the needle next to it. Then she covered them both with a blouse.

Melody started to cry. Cindy was still hurting, but she walked over and picked her up. Melody threw her arms around her mother and put her cheek against hers. Cindy could feel the hot tears. Then she began to quiver. She could feel Melody's grip tighten.

Melody needed security—a mother without fear. But Cindy's life was full of fear, and she could never give what she should give as a mother.

Cindy stared at the ceiling. She didn't even notice the fallen plaster. Would there ever be a time in her's and Melody's lives when they could be like other mothers and daughters? Could they ever move out of this dirty, filthy apartment? Was it possible to really find peace—lasting peace?

There must be an answer, but Cindy didn't know where or how.

Cindy carried Melody over to her bed and laid her down. She pulled the wrinkled covers up over her shoulders. Then she reached down and patted Melody's face.

Melody turned and looked the other way.

Exhausted and hurting, Cindy fell into her own bed. She closed her eyes, but sleep wouldn't come. Then she heard Melody slip out of the other bed and climb into hers.

"Mommy, are you afraid?"

"No, honey," Cindy lied.

Cindy felt Melody's arm reach around her neck and pull her close. "I love you, Mommy!"

Cindy rolled over and threw her arms around Melody. "Oh, my darling, I love you too. I just don't know what I'd ever do without you. You're the sweetest little girl any mother could have. You're all I've got!"

A big lump formed in her throat. Was it fair to subject the child to this kind of life? Cindy had to spend nights out there in the streets. She had to do something to support her drug habit. And now Mrs. Johnson had cut her off. What could they do?

It was a long night, but finally they both drifted off to a troubled sleep. About ten the next morning Cindy fixed a breakfast of dry cereal. Neither had much to say.

After breakfast Cindy told Melody, "I've got to go down to the corner to make a phone call. You stay here, and I'll be right back."

"Mommy, are you coming back? I get scared here by myself. You will come back, won't you?" Melody's face mirrored terror.

"Of course, darling. Mother won't be gone more than ten minutes."

Melody had been disappointed many times before. She took another spoonful of cereal.

When she reached the corner telephone, Cindy dialed child welfare and asked for Mrs. Shephard.

"This is Cindy Lippincot. I understand you stopped by yesterday to see me?"

"Yes, I did. We've been getting complaints that you've been leaving your daughter alone for quite some time. I think you should come down, and we should talk about it.''

"What do you mean, leaving her alone?" Cindy countered. "She's been with Mrs. Johnson."

"Not all the time, Cindy. We have reports that you've been leaving her there alone some nights. Do you realize how serious that is? What if a fire broke out? Furthermore, you don't know who could be knocking at the door. There's a bunch of perverted people in this city. If they knew Melody was alone, that would be it. I think you and I should talk about it.''

"Talk about what?"

"About Melody's future."

"What future? She's mine! She's *mine!* I won't give her up! Don't you understand? She's all I've got!" Cindy was screaming.

There was a long pause. "I didn't say I was going to take Melody away from you. I just said I think we should talk.''

"Okay, I'll come up and talk. But I'm not giving her up! No matter what!" Cindy slammed the receiver down.

"Come on, Melody. Mommy wants to get dressed. We're going to ride the subway."

Cindy tried to wash some of the grime off her daughter. Most of her dresses were dirty, and none of them were pressed. She tried to straighten one out as best she could.

"Where we going, Mommy?"

"To see a lady."

"Who, Mommy?"

"Oh, just a lady who wants to see us."

Melody was excited about the subway ride. But Cindy kept thinking: *Is it right to keep Melody? Is it selfish? Would she be better off staying with someone else? And it was true what Mrs. Shephard said— something terrible could happen.*

She pulled Melody closer to her. She wouldn't be able to live if something happened to Melody. She was all she had in life.

Melody looked up, sensing something was happening. "Is something bad going to . . .?"

"No, honey. Now don't worry. Nothing bad is going to happen."

They got off the subway and walked to 444 Madison Avenue. Inside they took the elevator to the fourth floor. Then they walked down the hall to the door that said BUREAU OF CHILD WELFARE. Cindy opened it.

"Hello, Mrs. Shephard. I came to talk."

"Thank you, Cindy. And, Melody, how are you today?"

She reached down for the child's hand.

Melody just stood there.

"I must inform you, Cindy, that this is a very serious thing. I have a court order concerning your daughter. Won't you please be seated?"

"No, I won't be seated!" Cindy shouted. "Just take good care of my daughter."

Before the startled social worker could respond, Cindy turned and leaped into the hallway. She slammed the door and ran to the elevator, sobbing as if her heart would break.

She heard Mrs. Shephard's door open. She was running toward her. *Oh, if that elevator would just get here! Where are the stairs?*

Fortunately the elevator arrived. Cindy jumped in.

"Mommy! Mommy! Please come back! Please don't leave me, Mommy." Melody was screaming as she ran toward the elevator.

Cindy saw the tears. Melody screamed out again, "Mommy! Mommy! Don't leave me! Don't leave me! Don't leave me! Mommy! Mommy! Come back! Don't leave me!"

Cindy knew it had to be this way—sudden and without any parting comment. The elevator door closed before Mrs. Shephard could reach it. Melody screamed again.

The world had just come to an end for Cindy Lippincot. Would she ever see Melody again?

The noise of the elevator as it labored toward the first floor drowned out the sound of those pitiful screams, but not the reality. What would poor Melody think? What would she think of her? Would she ever trust anyone again? Oh, why did it have to end like this?

4

Out on the street again, Cindy knew what she had to do. She'd done it many times before. And somehow she had to get Melody's screams out of her mind. So she headed toward Forty-eighth Street and Eighth Avenue. The best place in town to pick up a "john." Men were always willing to pay for a good time.

She was still sobbing, but now she was thinking. Would Melody really be cared for by Mrs. Shephard? Would she end up in the children's shelter? She read in the paper about that home where they put wayward children. It was crowded, undisciplined, and lacked supervision. Would Melody grow up to be a drug addict and prostitute like her mother?

Maybe they would place her in a foster home. Yes, that was it—a nice foster home for Melody. That would solve all the problems.

Then Cindy remembered Mr. and Mrs. Thomasson who took in foster children. When Cindy was twelve, she had become acquainted with one of their foster children. The memories still haunted her. She knew the only reason the Thomassons took in foster children was to make money. The state paid well, and this was how they supplemented their income. But they were mean! Would Melody end up in a home like that?

Yet it wasn't fair to Melody to try to take her back. Besides, Mrs. Shephard probably wouldn't ever give her back—not now anyway.

But what about Melody? How did *she* feel about it?

That last look at Melody before the elevator door closed her off forever was indelibly imprinted upon Cindy's mind. There was only one way to try to erase it—get high.

Almost before she realized it Cindy was at Forty-eighth Street and Eighth Avenue. With so many people around it should be easy for her to turn her first trick.

In a few minutes a well-dressed man walked by. Cindy moved right up next to him. "Want to have a good time?" she asked.

He kept walking.

Some men were like that. They were so scared they wouldn't even respond. She'd try another.

She kept her eye out for the right type. From years of experience she knew why men walked the streets. Some were sightseers, but some were out for other things.

She spotted a man coming toward her in a green leisure suit. He looked like the typical businessman who'd come to town for a convention. Cindy stepped right up to him.

"Want to have a good time?"

"What do you mean, a good time?"

"You know," Cindy said with a smile. "Have a good time."

"Sure!" Now the man was smiling.

"Okay, follow me," Cindy said.

She led the man down to Forty-eighth Street. There was a rundown hotel there that she often used. It was cheap.

"Just a minute, lady," the man said. "Are you sure this place is safe?"

Cindy laughed. "Don't worry, mister. My father owns this hotel."

"I don't believe you," he said. "I've heard about places like this, and I think I had just better walk on my way."

"You don't have to do that," Cindy purred. "Come on. You and I could have a good time. You know, just a date or something like that."

"Let's go through this once more," he said. "What do you mean by having a good time or by having a date?"

Cindy stared at him. "Come on, now. You're in New York and don't know what I mean by having a date or having a good time? Don't tell me you're an innocent little boy still on his mother's lap!"

"Please don't get me wrong," the man said. "I'm just in town purchasing some cars for my lot in South Carolina. I've been divorced for a couple of years, and I was just looking for someone to go out on a date with. I didn't intend to come to a place like this." He was indignant.

Cindy knew she had gotten hold of a real bummer—some stupid guy who didn't know where it was really at.

"Okay, mister, I'll level with you. When us girls in this town meet a guy like you, this business of having a date or going out means one thing. It means going to bed."

"You mean to tell me, when you saw me on that street over there, you were propositioning me? You were asking me to go to bed with you? For a price?"

"Yep. You said it. That's exactly what I was asking you."

"Well, I never . . . ." The man turned and started to leave. Then he raised one arm in the air, turned back, and grabbed Cindy.

"What's the big idea?"

"You're under arrest."

"Under arrest? Are you kidding? Who in the world do you think you are?" Cindy yelled.

The man reached into his vest pocket and flipped out his badge.

"I'll deny everything in court. It's your word against mine. There ain't no way you're going to get me this time," Cindy screamed.

"Calm down, sister, calm down. I've got everything you said on my recorder."

The detective pulled back his jacket a little farther. Strapped to his shoulder was a recording device. Next to it was his gun. Cindy knew you couldn't beat a gun or a recording device. They had her.

The detective reached to his back, pulled out his handcuffs, and deftly clamped them on Cindy. He had done that before.

In a few minutes a police car pulled up. One of the officers stepped out and reached for Cindy. "You got one! Good for you, Joe," he said. "The commissioner will be happy. He's still fuming about that one he missed yesterday."

"Hey, wait a minute, officer. I don't know what you're talking about. All I was doing was walking along the street, and this creep stopped me. I didn't say one word to him, and he walked up and propositioned me. It was his fault. The dirty, stinking little fink!"

The officer shrugged. "Come on, lady. Get in the back. Tell it to the judge."

Cindy stiffened. She started to jerk back.

"Come on, come on; don't give us a hard time." The officer gave her a shove. He pushed her all the way into the backseat and slammed the door.

Cindy couldn't keep back the tears as they headed toward the precinct. It was bad enough to lose Melody. Now she was heading toward jail. What could be worse?

At the Thirty-seventh Precinct they took her in, fingerprinted her, and put her in a cell. Later they took her down to be arraigned.

She was in the bull pen for that. That's where they kept the prisoners before bringing them to the judge. The idea of calling it the bull pen didn't come from the prisoners. That is what the cops called the people inside. They all acted like bulls.

In a few moments an officer took Cindy to the courtroom. She heard the court clerk say loudly, "Case number 465. Cindy Lippincot."

The officer marched her up in front of the judge. She glanced up. He was staring at her.

The court clerk continued to read: "Cindy Lippincot, you are hereby charged with violation of criminal code 230B—prostitution, a misdemeanor."

Cindy looked at the floor. The judge spoke. "I notice, young lady, that you have been in this court before."

Cindy continued to stare at the floor. It was true; she had been here before. In fact a couple of times it had been the same judge. She hoped he wouldn't recognize her. If he did, she was in real trouble. He would probably double the normal sentence.

"In fact you've been here ten times before. Is that right?"

Cindy was afraid to look up now. She continued to stare at the floor.

"Young lady, I'm speaking to you," the judge said sternly.

Then he shouted, "Look at me!"

Cindy slowly lifted her head and glared.

"That's better," the judge said, apparently not noticing her insolence.

Cindy abruptly dropped her head and continued to stare at the floor.

"Proceed," the judge said.

The next person to speak was George Benson, the assistant district attorney. Cindy knew Benson—a young kid on his way up. He got smart in court now and then, and Cindy hated him. But she knew enough not to mess around with him because he was very articulate. If you tried to challenge him, you always ended up with a tougher sentence. She decided it would be wise to cooperate.

"Do you understand that if you plead guilty to this charge, you waive your right to a trial by jury?" Benson asked. He continued rattling it off: "In so doing, you may be sentenced to six months in jail, or a five-hundred-dollar fine, or both."

Cindy raised her head and looked over at him. "Yes," she said. It was scarcely audible.

"Has anyone threatened you or made any promises if you plead guilty?"

"No."

"Do you plead guilty to the charge of prostitution, a B misdemeanor, punishable by six months in prison, or a fine of $500, or both?" he asked.

"Yes," Cindy answered. "Your Honor, I would

like to enter a plea of guilty.''

That was it—guilty. The road ahead was getting rougher—no turning back now.

The judge spoke. ''Young lady, I'll ask you once more. Do you fully understand what it means to plead guilty before this court?''

''Yes, Your Honor.''

Cindy waited. There was a long silence as the judge studied the documents before him. This was a moment of truth. If a judge liked you, he could suspend your sentence. If not, you were in real trouble. And Cindy somehow knew this time it would be the worst.

''Look up here, young lady.''

Cindy quickly jerked her head up. This was no time for games. This judge held her future in his hands. More silence.

''All right, then—six months.''

Cindy bowed her head. Six months—six months in the slammer!

It was no picnic to go to jail. Jails were horribly hot in the summer and deathly cold in the winter. The food was lousy, and that small cell gave you a feeling that the world was caving in on you. It seemed to keep getting smaller and smaller and smaller, until it was finally squeezing you like a vise, squeezing every ounce of motivation out of you.

She had been there before. Now she was going there again.

''Okay, lady, this way.'' The officer motioned her toward the door. Tomorrow it would be Rikers Island. Six months at Rikers Island!

The officer led her down a hall with cells arranged along the wall. He opened the door of the last cell.

There was no one else inside.

The clanging of the door behind her echoed back and forth over the bare walls. And in her head Cindy could still hear it clanging. It kept getting louder and louder.

Out of the horrible darkness she imagined a voice. She threw herself on the empty steel bed. There was that voice screaming out again and again, "Mommy! Mommy! Don't leave me! Don't leave me! Don't leave me!"

Deep in the recesses of her mind Cindy felt herself falling, falling, falling toward a deep, dark, horrible pit. Something was sucking her out to eternity. She was lost! She was lost! Lost! No more daughter. No more family communication. No one loved her. No one!

Cindy screamed at the top of her voice.

Her mind was playing tricks on her again. She remembered when it all started. Her parents tried to warn her, but she wouldn't listen.

It seemed like yesterday when she and her mother were in her bedroom. What a nice room it was. Cindy was getting ready to go out. Her mother was fussing about it.

"Oh, Mom, you don't have to worry about me. I can take care of myself."

"Yes, I'm sure you can, but a few of your friends seem to be a little too wild for their own good," her mother said.

"They're good kids, Mom. You just don't understand. Times have changed since you were growing up."

"Wait until you have children of your own, young lady. You'll worry too."

That was her mother—always worrying. Her mom and dad were nice, even if they seemed a little bit old-fashioned.

"Come on, Mom. Let's go downstairs. Daddy's probably hungry enough to eat a horse."

They walked down together to where her dad was waiting. Most of the time he was pretty nice. Oh, he did drink a little too much now and then. But there was one thing he really seemed to lack. He just didn't understand Cindy.

"Well, sweetheart, where are you off to today?"

"Some of the kids thought we might go over to Springfield to a rock concert," Cindy answered. She wasn't one to try to hide what she planned to do from her parents.

"I always worry about you in those surroundings," her mother said.

"Mother, really! I'm not a little girl anymore!"

"Honey, we know you aren't a child," her father said. "But a lot of unsavory things happen at those rock concerts. People get into trouble by going along with their friends who do things that aren't right or aren't good for them."

Then Mom jumped in. "Cindy, your father's right. The ladies in my club were talking about that last week. There always seems to be drugs at those concerts."

"Get off my back, Mom. I know enough. I'll never get involved with that stuff."

"Well, don't let anyone talk you into trying any of that junk," her father said. "It could ruin your life!"

"Ruin your life! Ruin your life! Ruin your life!" The

words reverberated again and again in her mind. Cindy came to. She looked up. Bars—she was in jail.

The next day they transferred her to Rikers Island. She decided the best thing to do would be to try to adjust, if there was such a thing.

That evening she lay down to try to sleep. Eventually she dozed off. She had another dream.

5

Cindy dreamed she was a teenager again sitting on the front steps of her home.

It was a kind of lazy Saturday afternoon. There was not really much to do. She was bored.

Usually on Saturday afternoons the kids gathered over at Johnny's Pizza Parlor. Johnny made good pizza, but the kids really went there to buy and sell drugs. Cindy loved the pizza. Now her folks had found out about the drugs, so no more Johnny's for her.

What's there to do in this dumb town? she wondered.

Just then a van pulled up. Not just any van. It was Sid's! He was a good-looking, redheaded football player who could get a vanload of girls anytime he wanted. But Cindy was a little suspicious of him. Rumor around school had it that he was on drugs.

There was Joe with him. He was Cindy's dreamboat. Wow! Were they really stopping here?

And Lyn—her name was Carolyn, but everybody called her Lyn. She was one of those who was everybody's friend.

Lyn leaned out the window and yelled, "Hey, Cindy! Want to go for a little ride? Or are you having too much fun sitting on the front steps?" Cindy could hear them all laughing.

"Not really. What are you up to?" Cindy yelled back.

"Ah, nothing. Just tooling around town having a

good time. We saw you sitting there. Want to come along with us?"

Of course she did. But should she take a chance with these three?

If they offer me drugs, I can refuse, she reasoned. *Why not go? I'm big enough to take care of myself. If they're fooling around with drugs, I can come back home.*

"I'm with you. Hang on till I tell my mom. I'll be right back!" Cindy yelled.

"Mom, I'm going for a ride with Lyn," Cindy said.

In moments she had run down the steps and to the van. Joe got out so she could sit between him and Sid. Wow! The van sure was beautiful! Carpeting all over the floor. Big, plush seats. And his music was overwhelming. No wonder all the girls wanted to ride in Sid's van.

As soon as Cindy hopped in she looked at the backseat. She had a sudden urge to get out right then. Barbara and Terry were back there, higher than a kite.

"Come on, Baby. We're going to have a good time," Joe yelled. Sid took off. It was too late now.

"What do you mean, have a good time? I thought we were just going for a ride," Cindy said.

"Yeah, that's all we're doing. Just driving around and staying cool," Sid said.

Cindy noticed the van weaving back and forth across the road. She reached down and grabbed the seat.

Joe stuck his hand in his pocket and pulled out two pills. He handed them to Cindy.

"What's this? You trying to get me hooked on pills?"

"Come on, Cindy. Just pop a couple of these, and you'll really groove."

Cindy shook her head and started to stare out the window.

"Hey, Baby—don't listen to all that garbage about getting hooked," Sid said. "I've been smoking pot and popping pills for years, and I can stop whenever I feel like it."

"Well, if you're so smart, why don't you stop then?" Cindy asked.

"Why should I? It makes me feel good. It even helps me drive better." Sid laughed.

The van lurched to the left. A car was coming. Sid swung back to the right. He was having difficulty keeping it on a straight course.

Cindy sat back and decided to make the best of it. After all, it was better than sitting on her front steps. Joe and Lyn kept cracking jokes. They certainly did seem to be having a great time.

"Are you sure I can't get hooked?" Cindy asked Sid.

Joe butted in. "Sure we're sure, Cindy. We're your friends, aren't we?"

Joe reached over and put his arms around Cindy. He drew her up close and smiled that big smile that would make any girl melt. "And you know how I feel about you, Baby. Come on. Just pop a couple and join us. See what I'm talking about."

Did Joe really mean what he was saying? Who cares? She was snuggled up next to him now! And she'd always wondered what it would be like to be high.

She reached out and grabbed the two pills and

popped them into her mouth.

"Hey, that's more like it, Cindy! Now you'll really be with it!" Joe squeezed her again.

In a few minutes Cindy felt dizzy. Then all of a sudden she felt very light—rising higher and higher. Oh, oh! This felt so good!

The rest of them had started singing. Cindy joined in. She never had been much of a singer, but it sounded so right to sing along with them. Yes, they were right. This did feel good.

She glanced out the windshield and screamed. Sid was on the wrong side of the road, and they were headed straight for that semi. She heard brakes screeching, glass cracking, metal tearing apart. There were more screams, moans, blood, hurting—hurting . . . .

Cindy awoke screaming at the top of her voice. She was still in prison.

Now she couldn't sleep. The dream brought back that flood of memories of how foolish she had been in starting on drugs. She was so innocent, so gullible. It took just two pills.

That first step became a living nightmare. She could still clearly remember waking up in the hospital after that horrible accident. The others had been hurt too. Sid died.

After that, whenever Cindy got into any kind of pressure situation, she turned to drugs. Joe and Lyn gave up drugs, but Cindy continued. And now this was where it had landed her—in jail again.

Cindy served the six months as best she could. There was no such thing as getting used to jail life, but she tried not to rock the boat or make waves.

When the long six months finally ended, they released her. At ten that morning they walked her to the front door. Without saying good-bye or even looking around, Cindy walked down the steps. She was free again.

But as with most people who get out of jail, there was no job to go to. About the only thing an ex-prisoner has is the clothes on his back. He faces harsh realities. No job, no money, and his only friends are the ones he knew in the streets. And they are hardly friends.

Cindy had faced this before too. And she knew of only one thing to do. Not that she wanted to; she had to. She would go back to Forty-eighth Street and Eighth Avenue. She could turn another trick to get some money. Money would buy her drugs. Drugs would help her forget.

When she got to Forty-eighth Street, she knew something was wrong. There were cops all over the place. She wasn't about to solicit anybody under those conditions.

She took the subway to Twenty-third Street. There were cops all around there too. *Another big crackdown?* she wondered. She had heard about the police commissioner's project when she was in jail. *Is he still on his rampage? Things haven't changed much since I got sent up!*

She got back on the subway. This time Cindy went up to Fifty-seventh Street and Avenue of the Americas. It was next to the Hilton Hotel. She'd never solicited there before but heard it was a good place because of the businessmen. She started walking up and down the street, smiling at the men.

One man in particular looked very inviting. She went up and asked him if he wanted to have a good time.

"For crying out loud, lady, you just solicited a policeman." He reached into his side pocket and flipped out his badge.

"Oh, no!" Cindy cried. "I just got out of jail this morning. Now you're going to bust me and send me back?" Cindy was petrified. She couldn't think of anything worse.

"I'll make a deal with you," the officer said. "Get off the street right away, and I'll move on. I'm on another case, and I don't have time to take you down to the precinct. Is that a bargain?"

"You bet it is!" Cindy said. "I'm long gone already."

She didn't even look back as she ran down the street. Junkies just didn't get breaks like this. Maybe her luck was going to change!

Three blocks later she slowed down. She turned around and looked toward the Hilton. No cops in sight. She drew a deep breath.

She turned the corner and started to walk over to Eighth Avenue. Then she spotted him. Leaning up against a building just ahead was her special friend, Monty—what luck! She had run into her pusher. Things were looking up!

"Hi, Monty. How's things going?"

"Just fine. How about you? Haven't seen you lately."

It was all double-talk. But it was normal. All Cindy

wanted from Monty was drugs. All Monty wanted from Cindy was money. Just a very simple transaction.

"Monty, I'm jammed up tight. I just got out of jail, and I need a bag to set me up. Can you give me a bag?"

"Just a bag?" Monty retorted sarcastically. "Of course, just a bag. But it's going to cost ya fifteen dollars. Or I'll strike a deal with ya. I'll give ya two bags for twenty-five dollars. How's that?"

"Quit fooling around, Monty. I just got out of jail doing six months, and I ask you for a little favor. I'm not asking you for ten bags or five bags, but just one bag. As soon as I'm up to it, I'll turn a trick and pay you."

"Hey, Cindy baby. Don't hassle me. You know I run a strictly cash-and-carry business. No credit."

"Please, Monty, just let me get off this once, and I'll get out on the street. You'll get paid. Trust me."

"Listen, Baby—you pay cash, just like everyone else. You hear me? Besides, I'm not carrying anything."

Cindy grabbed his lapels and pulled him toward her. "I know you keep some stashed in your room. Let's go up there; I promise you'll be well paid. Know what I mean?"

Monty pulled her hands from his coat. "Okay, but this is the last time."

Monty was a real smart pusher who lived with his mother, Mrs. Henderson. She knew nothing about his drug dealing.

As Monty and Cindy walked along together, the telephone rang in Mrs. Henderson's apartment. It was Maude from Lou's Bakery.

"Mrs. Henderson, I don't mean to butt into your

business, but I thought there was something you should know."

"What are you talking about? What should I know?" Mrs. Henderson demanded.

"Well, I just saw your Monty with a girl who is a prostitute and a drug addict."

"My son with a prostitute? I don't believe it. Monty's a good boy. He wouldn't be up to no good with a prostitute."

"Well, Mrs. Henderson, they were walking along the street in front of the bakery. They looked as though they might be headed for your place. I thought you should know."

"Headed towards here? My goodness. You don't think they would use my place for something bad, do you?"

"If I were you, I would do something to keep your boy away from that immoral girl!"

With the receiver still in her hand, Mrs. Henderson looked out her window. She gasped.

"Is the girl you're talking about wearing a red skirt and a white blouse?"

"That's the one."

"From here I can see Monty, and sure as anything, there is a girl with him wearing a red skirt and a white blouse."

"That's her. That's that bad girl I was telling you about. She's no good for Monty!"

"Thanks, Maude. I'll take care of it."

Mrs. Henderson walked away from the window. "God help me. Whatever am I going to do?"

She didn't have long to wait. Monty pushed the door open and followed Cindy in. They were both laughing.

Monty jumped when he saw his mother.

"Oh, hi, Mom. I thought you'd be over at Aunt Joan's house."

Deathly silence lay over the room. Mrs. Henderson kept staring at Cindy.

"Mom, this is my friend Cindy. Cindy, this is my mom, Mrs. Henderson."

Cindy stepped forward and held out her hand. "Hi, Mrs. Henderson. Nice to meet you."

Mrs. Henderson nodded coolly.

"Uh, Mom, we just thought we'd come up for a drink of water. Okay?"

"Of course. It's your home too."

"Come on, Cindy. Let's go into the kitchen."

When Monty turned on the water full force, Cindy whispered, "How can we get rid of your old lady? She doesn't know you're a pusher, does she?"

Monty put his fingers to his lips. "She's liable to hear you!"

Cindy put her hands on her hips. She wanted to get this over with and get her drugs and get out of there. "Get rid of her," she ordered.

"Not so fast, Cindy. You're not in much of a position to be giving orders around here. Just wait a minute. I'll think of something."

Just then Mrs. Henderson walked into the kitchen.

"Monty, there's something I want to say to you, and I want to say it in front of your friend."

"Sure, Mom. What is it?"

Mrs. Henderson glared at Cindy. "Did you know that your friend here is a very bad girl?"

"Who, Cindy? Aw, come on. You've got to be kidding!"

"In plain language, son, she's a prostitute and a drug addict!"

Cindy jerked and stared at Mrs. Henderson.

"How can you say that, Mom? You don't even know her."

Before anyone knew what was happening, Mrs. Henderson reached over and grabbed Cindy's arm. She jerked it toward Monty and pointed at the needle marks. "Look!" she said triumphantly. "Do you know what these black marks are?"

Cindy jerked away. Monty turned his head.

Cindy hadn't said anything yet, but she was raging on the inside. The humiliation of being put down like this!

"She's a dirty, good-for-nothing junkie," Mrs. Henderson burst out. "Get her out of here!"

"Come on, Mom. Don't say that."

"I said get that rotten tramp out of my house," Mrs. Henderson screamed.

She walked over and stood in front of Cindy, her face only six inches away from Cindy's. She screamed again, even louder, "I said get out of my house, you slut!"

It was more than Cindy could stand. She reared back and slapped Mrs. Henderson across her face. Blood trickled from her mouth. Cindy raised her hand to strike again, but Monty stepped in and stopped her.

"I'll kill her! I'll kill her! I'll kill her!" Cindy screamed. "No one's going to talk about me like that!"

Monty was pushing her toward the door.

"Did you see that, Monty? She struck me. I'm bleeding! Get her out of here now! She's no good!

She'll ruin you, and you'll end up just like her—a bum!"

Monty finally got the apartment door open and pushed Cindy out, following her.

As he reached back to shut the door, his mother yelled again, "I never want to see you with that girl again! Do you understand?"

Out in the hallway, Monty stopped. "Look, Baby, you know you almost got me in trouble? You blew it. If Mom calls the cops on you, we're both in real trouble."

"What do you mean, call the cops? You heard your mother and the way she treated me. What I should have done was grabbed her by the neck and strangled her. You're just lucky I didn't kill her!"

"What are you trying to say to me, Cindy? You want to kill my mother? I do you a favor, and you want to kill my mother. Is that what you're saying?"

"That's exactly what I'm saying. I ought to go back in there and bust her head against the wall."

"I'll tell you what you can do, Cindy. See that door at the bottom of the steps? I'll give you three seconds to get down there and out that door. If you're not gone in three seconds, I'm going to pick you up, put you over my head, and throw you down there. You're going to end up at the bottom all crumpled and messy. Then I'll call the cops to come and get you. And they'll bust you. Instead of six months, you're going to get six years. I'm going to charge you with soliciting, unlawful entry, and assault with intent to kill. You know what I mean?"

Cindy knew better than to mess with Monty. She had known other girls who had double-crossed him.

He was counting, "One . . . ."

There was only one thing to do—get out of there. Now!

Cindy made record time down those stairs. Outside she waited to hear if Monty's footsteps were following. There was nothing. She headed toward Fifty-second Street.

What happened to that streak of luck? she wondered. Things were now going from bad to worse. And Cindy stil! had no drugs.

A patter of rain—then another. Soon it was pelting down. "Just what I need," Cindy muttered. "This will chase all the 'johns' off the streets. Now what am I going to do?"

She just kept walking. She didn't know how far. And she didn't know where her walk was going to take her!

6

Cindy hardly noticed the rain as she walked now. What was the point in stopping? Where was there to go anyhow? Into a coffeeshop for shelter? Stand in the doorway of some tenement house and gag with the stench?

By this time her directionless walk had taken her toward the East Side.

She "happened" by a storefront church and heard beautiful singing. She stopped. It was a choir. Sounded like all women's voices. So she stepped inside.

Cindy glanced toward the front of the small church. About fifteen girls dressed in blue were singing. My, they looked happy! She'd never been in a church like this before. Who were they?

About seventy-five people were there—old people, young people, children, families. They all seemed intent on listening to this choir.

It's better than being out in the rain, Cindy decided. She spotted a vacant pew at the back. As she sat down, she noticed a woman glance in her direction.

The choir finished its song. It was something about meeting the Master. *Who could that be?* she wondered. *Certainly not a pimp!*

The girl playing the piano addressed the audience. "Yes, Christ will touch your life, if only you'll let Him. And now I'd like for Saundra Lozinski to tell you what Christ has done in her life."

This certainly was a different kind of church service.

What was a *girl* doing speaking in church? Only men were supposed to do that.

Saundra was rather petite. Cindy wondered what she would have to say. *She probably doesn't have the faintest idea what life's all about,* Cindy decided.

"I started using drugs when I was fourteen, and I used them for seven years," Saundra began. "I was arrested five times for possession."

Cindy could hardly believe what she was hearing. She edged forward. Why would this girl named Saundra start off by telling these church people that she was a drug addict?

Cindy watched intently. Was she still on drugs? There was such a wonderful glow to her face—she must have beaten her habit. How did she ever do that?

"I did anything to support my habit," Saundra continued, "and I do mean *anything*. I guess the worst I ever felt was when I was kicking drugs cold turkey in an isolation cell."

This girl has been around. I wonder if she is for real?

"In isolation I was totally abandoned. Nobody came to talk or to ease my cramps or to bring me down easy with methadone. There was no one to offer a helping hand."

Cindy could identify with that. She recalled when she had to kick cold turkey in jail. She had that big army-type blanket around her, but she was still freezing to death. She rolled from side to side on that wooden cell bed.

She remembered clutching her stomach to ease the pain. That dark, dingy cell was no comfort. That dirty little sink and toilet bowl and the bed were the only furniture or seat she had. That was the worst place in the world to try to kick your habit. And those prison bars felt like tentacles strangling you.

The more Cindy thought about it, the harder she gritted her teeth. Saundra's voice brought her back to reality.

"You keep feeling like vomiting, but nothing comes up. Your heaving gets so bad that your whole gut feels like it's going to tear apart . . . ."

It seemed like Saundra was reliving Cindy's life!

Cindy remembered that cold sweat she had in that jail cell and getting up and heading for the toilet. Over the toilet she had only dry heaves. She staggered back to her cot and tried to lie down to ease the pain.

She would clutch her head while kicking there in the cell. Periodically she rubbed her legs. It was only a momentary relief. The pain, and it was so intense, came back.

She never would forget the time that, after rolling from side to side, she had vomited all over the floor. Then she looked up. There was the matron at the cell door.

She never forgot what that comforting, soothing matron shouted at her: "Clean up that mess!"

Cindy was totally exhausted. In her agony she had screamed back, "I'm not cleaning up anything! I'm sick!"

Cindy had waited for the matron to unlock the door and to push her face into her vomit. She knew of other girls that had happened to.

This time the matron turned and walked down the hall. Cindy had breathed a sigh of relief, but the stench from the vomit was overwhelming. And she was too sick to clean it up.

Cindy remembered getting up slowly and walking over to the sink. She washed her face with cold water. As she looked up at her face she couldn't believe what she saw. It looked like a ninety-year-old woman. Her eyes were sunken. They had dark bags under them. Her hair was a mess. If this was the price to pay for being a drug addict, it wasn't worth it.

It wasn't as though she had never asked for help. She remembered the time she had gone home to kick. Her parents let her back in. And in her agony she remembered rolling on the front-room couch.

The intense pain was overwhelming. Cindy's parents decided to call Pastor Schwartz. He came immediately.

Kneeling next to Cindy, he had said, "My dear, we just want to help you. Your parents love you very much."

Cindy's mother sat on the edge of the couch, weeping. She blurted out, "We just can't sit by and watch while you destroy your life with drugs."

And Cindy remembered looking up at her father and seeing the pain on his face as he said, "Cindy, you're all we have. Everything we've done is for you and your future!"

Cindy hadn't wanted to cause her parents all this anguish, and she cried out, "Please forgive me! I just can't help myself!"

Pastor Schwartz in his loving way said, "That's why we want to help you."

"You just don't understand," Cindy had replied, "but I can't stop . . . . It hurts too much when I try!"

Cindy's parents had put their arms around her again,

crying. The moment was so overwhelming. "Oh, Mama . . . Daddy . . . it's better if I just go away!"

Cindy felt hot tears flowing. She reached up to wipe them. It brought her back to where she was—in church. Saundra was still speaking.

"I used to go into the hospital where they kept me doped up, just to get my habit down to where I could support it with no sweat.

"It was while I was in that cell that I decided: I'm not going to spend the rest of my life in and out of jail and finally end up like every other junkie—just skin and bones with half of my teeth knocked out!"

Cindy knew what Saundra was talking about. That thought had crossed her mind every day for the past six years. Where would she end up?

Saundra continued, "After a week of living hell in that cell, I was taken to court. As I walked in, I saw my lawyer talking to the judge, my probation officer, and a couple of other men. The judge looked like he was going to give me three to five without batting an eye. Boy, was I scared!

"The more the judge and the others shook their heads, the more scared I got!

"Finally after what seemed like hours, the judge called me over to the bench. He told me he had agreed to give me a chance to straighten out my life—that I was to spend the next year at the Walter Hoving Home. That's the Teen Challenge girls' home. I was being paroled in their custody.

"Well, after a few weeks at the Home, I realized it wasn't what I had expected. I mean, I had had plenty of the Bible and Christ when I was growing up, but not the way the staff at the Home handled it.

"I did what I was told and slowly got into reading the Bible. Then one night, while reading the Bible, it hit me like a ton of bricks."

So this was it! Could Jesus and religion and the Bible really have changed Saundra? Was it really true?

Saundra looked around at the audience. By this time some had tears rolling from their eyes. This story was almost too good to be true!

But Cindy wasn't swallowing it all—not yet.

"Jesus suffered and died because of *my* sins, not just the sins of others," Saundra continued. "He died on the cross for me! The sins of the world were mine. I started crying and just broke down completely. It was beautiful—my own personal miracle! I cried out, 'Lord, I can't go on the way I've been. I know you're there; so please help me, God! Help me!'

"I cried and cried, and the tears helped wash away my old life. The Lord came in. I've been a new person ever since. Jesus set me free—truly free. He wants to do the same for you."

Cindy had heard enough. *Maybe for you, sister, but not for me. I'm a lost cause. Nobody can help me!* With those thoughts she headed toward the back door. It might have happened to Saundra, but it would never happen to her. For her the day of miracles was over!

It was still drizzling as Cindy hit the street, but she hardly noticed. There was only one thing for her to do, and she had to do it quickly.

She headed back toward her tenement apartment. Would her stuff still be there?

Her apartment looked even dirtier and filthier than when she had left it. Roaches scattered. A rat scurried out of sight. She didn't notice. Her mind was on one thing: not on a trick, not on getting off, something else . . . .

She opened the top drawer of the dresser and pushed back a blouse. The gun was still there! She reached back farther. Good! The bullets were there too. Nervously she loaded the gun and placed it atop the dresser.

It would take courage to pull the trigger. Could she do it? She walked over to the bed to think.

What would death be like? Did death really end it all? Or would she go to hell? And if she did, would it be worse than what life was now?

Then she thought of Melody. Sweet, darling little Melody. Where was she on this miserable, rainy day? Melody had always seemed to be so understanding. If she could only be here now. Maybe they could find a way out together.

But now there was no one here to comfort her. No one to talk to.

Yes, she would do it. No one would miss her. In slow, measured steps she moved toward the gun. Then she walked back to the bed—again she went toward the gun. This time she picked it up. *Funny how my hands tremble,* she thought. She walked back to the bed to steady herself.

She had read about many suicides. The girls had talked about them. Then there was her friend Martha. She had put a gun to her head, but somehow the bullet ricocheted off her skull. Martha recovered, but she spent most of her time in mental institutions. A vegetable, someone called her. Cindy shuddered.

She gripped the handle tighter. Deliberately she raised the gun to her head. She cocked the trigger and gritted her teeth. Tomorrow she would be just another statistic.

Suddenly someone knocked at the door. It startled Cindy so that she quickly lowered the gun and pushed it under the covers.

Who could that be? The knock came again—louder.

"Who's there?"

"It's Mrs. Redfield and Pastor Ryan from the church. We'd like to talk to you for a minute."

From the church? What church?

Cindy reached to push more covers over the gun. But unknowingly she pushed too far, and the gun was laying there in plain view. She walked shakily to the door and opened it slowly.

"I saw you sitting in church a few moments ago, and you looked so troubled," Mrs. Redfield began. "I found out where you live and brought the pastor to see if we could help."

Cindy recognized the woman. She was the one who was sitting a few feet away and had turned to glance at her a few times. And the young man standing next to her certainly looked compassionate.

"Is something wrong?" Pastor Ryan asked.

"We'd really like to help you, Cindy," Mrs. Redfield offered.

"Help? I don't need any help. I . . . I . . . ." She started to sob. She needed help more than anybody in the world. She was only one breath away from death!

Mrs. Redfield reached over, put her arm around Cindy, and drew her close to herself.

"Please come in," Cindy finally said through her sobs. Maybe there was help. Maybe someone really cared.

Cindy motioned the pastor to a chair—the only chair in the room. She asked Mrs. Redfield if she would mind sitting on the bed, and Cindy sat beside her.

As Mrs. Redfield sat down, she noticed the gun. She said nothing, but she slid her foot the other way.

"How long have you been on drugs?" Mrs. Redfield asked.

"Who told you I was on drugs?" Cindy countered defensively.

"My sister was an addict for nine years. I can spot one a mile away."

"What happened to your sister?"

Cindy always expected the worst from drug addicts. She had never met an old addict. Most of them either died from overdosing or ended up in obscurity in a prison or some place like that. All of them were somehow forgotten.

"Oh, that's a wonderful story," Mrs. Redfield said. "She went to the Walter Hoving Home, and Christ freed her from her drug habit."

"What's the Walter Hoving Home? Isn't that what the girl at church mentioned?"

"Right!" Pastor Ryan exclaimed. "It's a Teen Challenge girls' home in Garrison. A lot of girls find help there. In fact the choir you heard was from the Home."

So that's why it was such an unusual church service. I knew there was something different about that church.

"Well,.I really need help, Pastor. See that gun over there?" Cindy pointed. "Believe me, you saved my life. If you hadn't come . . . ." Her voice trailed off as if it were too hard to say it. She choked and then started again. "Yes, I really do need help. But I think it's too late. Honestly, Pastor, I don't know where help could ever come from!"

"Have you ever thought of reaching out to Christ for help?"

"How do I do that?"

The pastor scooted his chair closer. "Let me show you." He pulled a booklet from his pocket. "Have you ever heard of the Four Spiritual Laws?"

"Four Spiritual Laws?"

"There are physical laws that govern the universe," the pastor explained. "And there are also spiritual laws that govern our relationship with God."

"I know plenty about breaking the law, but I never heard about breaking God's law."

"Let me quickly share God's Four Spiritual Laws."

"I'm ready for anything."

"Law number one is that God loves you and has a wonderful plan for your life. In fact Christ said that He came so you could have life and have it abundantly. Cindy, why do you think that most people aren't experiencing abundant life?"

"I don't know. I didn't think anybody could."

"It's because of law number two," Pastor Ryan continued. "Man is sinful and separated from God. Thus he cannot know and experience God's love and plan for his life. Have you ever felt like a sinner?"

"Are you kidding? Sure I have. But I always kind of laughed at sin, like it was something you did when you stole cookies from the cookie jar."

"Well, that might be true, but sin is more serious than that," the pastor said.

"Sin is separation from God, which brings us to law

number three. Jesus Christ is God's only provision for man's sin. Through Him you can know and experience God's love and plan for your life."

Cindy wasn't all that convinced. Was the pastor trying to give her a snow job or was he for real? Certainly Saundra's testimony had sounded convincing, but it would be hard for Cindy to believe that Christ really cared about *her*.

"You mean that I can actually experience God's love and that He has a plan for my life?"

"That's absolutely true. And that brings us to law number four: We must individually receive Jesus Christ as our Saviour and Lord. Only then can we experience God's love and plan for our lives."

There was a long silence. In her mind Cindy was going over what the pastor had said. The only way a person could know and experience God's love was to receive Jesus as Saviour and Lord—and that was a very personal matter.

Finally the pastor spoke again, "Cindy, you receive Christ by turning to God. Trust in Christ, and He will come into your life, forgive you of your sins, and make you what He wants you to be."

Cindy hesitated. "I want to. I really do. But I guess I'm not quite ready. It's all so new. I'm . . . ."

Mrs. Redfield interrupted. "I know how you feel, Cindy. Before we came over, I spoke to one of the staff at the Walter Hoving Home, and they told me to bring you up. They said they'd be glad to help you."

The pastor reached over and touched Cindy's clenched hand. "Mrs. Redfield will take you there right now, if you want. Would you like to go?"

Cindy knew she didn't have anything to lose. She

really didn't have anything—period.

"I'll do anything you folks and God want me to do."

Pastor Ryan and Mrs. Redfield stood. Cindy got up slowly. At that instant someone banged loudly on the door.

"Open up in there, or we'll bust the door down!"

Cindy recognized that voice. It was Jimmy, the pimp. Cindy dove under the bed. Jimmy was out to kill her. And a pastor and a dear lady from his church wouldn't be much protection!

7

"Come on, Cindy baby. We know you're in there!" Ben yelled.

Cindy scooted from under the bed and headed toward the window. Jerking it open, she stuck one leg over the sill.

Pastor Ryan grabbed her shoulders. "What are you trying to do—kill yourself?"

"I have no choice. The last time these two gorillas had me, they almost killed me. This time it won't be *almost!*"

"Well, take a long, hard look down," Pastor Ryan whispered. "I guarantee that when you hit the ground, you're not going to bounce!"

With that he pulled her back in. "This is the time for us to keep a strong faith in the Lord," he said. "God will deliver us."

Ben yelled again. "I'm giving you five seconds, Cindy, and only five. I'm counting now. One, two, three . . . ."

Mrs. Redfield looked at the pastor. He put his fingers to his lips. Maybe the two hadn't heard them.

". . . five! Okay, Baby, the hard way!"

With a groan and a crash the door gave way. The two pimps lunged toward Cindy. Pastor Ryan stepped into their path.

"Hey! What's goin' on here?" Ben looked stunned. "Is this one of your 'johns'?"

"I'm Pastor Ryan. Cindy needs help. Can't you understand that?"

"Help, my eye!" Ben spit out the words as he pushed the pastor out of his way. "I'm going to give that little girl all the help she can stand! She's mine! You can't have her!"

The pastor grabbed Ben's arm.

"Not so fast, preacher!" Ben yelled as he yanked away. "I ain't got no use for preachers either."

Mrs. Redfield saw her chance, grabbed the gun, and pointed it unsteadily at Jimmy.

"Come on, lady. That thing ain't loaded."

She aimed at Jimmy's shoulder, trembling so hard she could scarcely keep the weapon straight.

Jimmy started toward her. Whang! The bullet zipped past him and splattered into the doorsill.

Jimmy ducked, moving his hands in a calming manner. "Okay, ma'am; we don't want no trouble. Just cool it with that thing!"

"I will," Mrs. Redfield snapped, "if you two just step aside and let us out."

Jimmy and Ben jumped back. Mrs. Redfield held the gun on them as Pastor Ryan and Cindy hurried out. Then she backed into the hall, the gun still pointed at the two pimps—their hands outstretched defensively.

She raised the gun as though to shoot again. Jimmy and Ben jerked their hands high over their heads. "And don't you try to follow us for fifteen minutes, or I won't just shoot at your shoulder!"

As the three moved quickly down the stairs Mrs. Redfield glanced back to see if they were being followed. Not a sound!

Pastor Ryan hurried Cindy to Mrs. Redfield's car. Right behind it was the pimpmobile—a gleaming white Cadillac with silver ornaments.

"That's their car," Cindy said nervously. "Do you think they'll follow us?"

Mrs. Redfield turned toward the pimpmobile, still clutching the gun. Deliberately she moved closer and pointed at the right front tire. She squeezed the trigger. The tire splattered with a great hiss, and the car lurched downward.

She walked over to the left front tire. She pointed the gun again. This time she closed her eyes. Again a loud bang, a hiss, and that side of the car descended.

Pastor Ryan was aghast. But his smile returned quickly. "They won't be following anybody for quite a while, will they?"

In triumph Mrs. Redfield raised the barrel of the gun near her mouth, blew the smoke away, and stuck the gun into her purse.

Pastor Ryan walked over to Cindy. "God has delivered you from those two pimps," he said. "Of course, Mrs. Redfield helped God out a little! But this is one more way that God is trying to show you that He loves you. I do hope you believe now that God really wants to deliver you from drugs. I know He does, and you will always have our prayers."

"Thanks, Pastor. I'll do my best."

Pulling away from the curb, Mrs. Redfield and Cindy headed upstate to Garrison, New York, and the Walter Hoving Home.

The pastor, however, had just started down the street when Ben and Jimmy burst out the front door of the tenement, running toward their car. Then they noticed the deflated tires. The air was blue with their angry comments!

Pastor Ryan hurried on his way. He decided it was best not to interfere in that one!

The thoughts of the past few moments rushed through his mind. It was thrilling to help Cindy and to save her from suicide and from the pimps. But would she stick it out at the Home? And what about the two pimps? God loved them too. Was there some way to help them?

8

The Walter Hoving Home is a beautiful twenty-three-acre estate located about forty miles north of New York City on the Hudson River. Girls aged twelve to forty-seven come to Garrison from various parts of the United States with problems of addiction, alcoholism, delinquency, and similar serious things. About fifty-five girls are in the one-year program at a time.

Cindy didn't have much to say on the way up. How could she? She really didn't know what she was facing. And she was still shaken up by that brush with the pimps.

Mrs. Redfield sensed her uneasiness and tried to explain what would happen at the Home. "During the mornings they have Bible classes," she said, "and during the afternoons there is a varied work program. And ninety percent of the girls who complete the program never go back to the problem they came with!"

"Do you mean their cure rate is ninety percent?" Cindy asked skeptically. "I've never heard of anything that even comes close to that!"

"The difference here is Jesus," Mrs. Redfield explained. "It's amazing what He can do. Believe me, their cure rate would be one hundred percent if all the girls continued to serve Jesus." She glanced over at Cindy. "There's no problem too hard for the Lord, Cindy. Always remember that. The problem He has is that people don't seem to understand Him or are not willing to accept Him. He can only do for them what they'll let Him do."

"Well, I'm certainly ready for a change!"

"You may not believe this, Cindy, but did you know that with the Lord it's easier to succeed than to fail? A lot of people don't know that. But I think you do. You realize how hard it is out on the street working for the devil."

"Working for the devil? I didn't know I was."

Mrs. Redfield chuckled. "Just think about it. You know, as a drug addict you never get a vacation or days off. You have to work every day, every week, every month, every year. And there is enormous danger in trying to support your habit. Right?"

"I never thought of it that way before, but I guess you're right. It *is* tough working for the devil."

Mrs. Redfield chuckled again. "Now let me tell you more about the Home, Cindy. It's not easy up there. They believe in discipline and that discipline brings security.

"You know how it is. If you properly spank a child, that child will throw her arms around you afterwards. Proper discipline brings security. That's what they believe at the Home. And they don't take any nonsense. They are for real, and they want to make sure every girl makes it through their program."

Just the mention of the word *child* sent Cindy's mind reeling back to Melody. Where was she now? How was she doing? Would she ever see her again?

"What happens after the girls graduate?" Cindy asked.

"Many of them go on for further schooling. Some have become staff members at the Home. Others go back to their families or are reunited with their children.''

"You mean I might get my daughter, Melody, back?'' Cindy had thought that was too much to even hope for.

"Of course, Cindy. One of the things God wants to do is to reunite you with your child.''

"But would the courts give Melody back to me?''

"I'll tell you my experience with the courts where children are concerned. If a judge is satisfied that the child will be well cared for, he'll give the child back to the mother. They've had a lot of cases like this at the Home, and, believe me, the courts have been most cooperative.

"In fact, one of the girls had been separated from her child for twelve years. This child was raised in a lot of institutions because the mother was an addict and unable to care for her. Now they are both living together. It's really a beautiful sight to see what God has done for both of them!''

Hope began to leap in Cindy's heart. Any sacrifice would be worth it if she could get Melody back.

Mrs. Redfield seemed to sense what she was thinking. "But let's get first things first, Cindy. The most important thing is to surrender your life and everything you have to the Lord. Then as you turn everything to Him, He has promised to direct your paths. Believe me, God knows what's best. In His timing He will bring Melody back to you. I believe that!''

"Oh, Mrs. Redfield. Just talking to you makes me feel so much better. I just hope it's all going to be true!''

"It *is* going to be true,'' she assured her. "In fact

that girl I just mentioned to you—you may know her. She used to hang around in your area. Her name is Raquel Colfax.''

"Raquel Colfax? Sure, I know her. We used to get off together! Somehow she came up missing. Someone said she'd died of an overdose. Do you mean she went up to the Walter Hoving Home?''

"I sure do. Raquel and her daughter, Sophia, are lovely Christian people. They now attend Calvary Tabernacle Church in Brooklyn.''

"I just can't believe it!''

"Like I'm trying to tell you, Cindy, nothing is too hard for the Lord!''

"I still remember when Raquel used to talk about her daughter. She would break down and cry—she missed her so much. And think of it! She's back with her daughter! That's absolutely beautiful! Beautiful!''

Things seemed brighter and brighter as she talked to Mrs. Redfield. *Will the Walter Hoving Home be as exciting as this?* she wondered.

It wasn't long before she found out.

After they reached Garrison they drove up the long, beautifully landscaped driveway to the main house, a three-story English Tudor mansion. Mrs. Redfield was right. It was breathtaking!

Inside, Shirley Swarthout, director of rehabilitation, welcomed them. "We've been hoping you'd come, Cindy,'' she said. "I believe God wants to do some wonderful things for you.''

Shirley explained the program, and they filled out the entrance forms. To Cindy's surprise, not once did Shirley try to discourage her. She seemed so hopeful that Cindy was going to make it.

Now Mrs. Redfield was leaving. "I'll be praying for

you, Cindy. You know, you're not the first girl I've brought up here. The others have succeeded. You can too!"

Cindy's eyes brimmed with tears as she said good-bye to her new friend.

That first week wasn't easy. Cindy quit counting the times she was ready to leave. Everything seemed so strange: the Bible classes, the work program. But day after day she began to believe that God had planned a glorious future for her.

One Sunday afternoon, however, she became terribly depressed. She felt good physically and thought maybe she could make it on the outside now. She remembered what Mrs. Redfield said about the courts. Maybe a judge would be sympathetic, and she could get Melody back. They could make a new start. With Melody back everything would turn out right!

When she told Shirley she was leaving, Shirley didn't wince. She called in one of the other girls.

"Monique," she said, "Cindy wants to leave. You know what that's like, don't you?"

Monique had been at the Home almost twelve months now and was ready to graduate. But many times she too had had to fight the temptation to leave.

"Why don't you take Cindy down by the pool, Monique? And, Cindy, I want Monique to tell you some of the temptations she has had to overcome. Maybe it'll help you think again about how important it is to stick it out here."

"I'll be glad to share with Cindy," Monique said. "In fact, Shirley, I can still remember the time you had Angie talk to me when I was going to leave. Remember?"

"Of course! That's why I asked you. And now you get the privilege of helping someone else as you have been helped!"

Monique and Cindy sat by the pool. The splashing waterfall gave an aura of serenity.

"About a year ago I was riding back and forth on the ferry from Staten Island to Manhattan," Monique began. "It was about ten-thirty on a Friday night, and I was looking for a girl who had stolen drugs from me in the past. I was going to kill her."

Cindy looked at Monique unbelievingly. She was only about five feet tall. She really must have been mad to have thought of murdering someone.

"Did you kill her?"

"No, and I really think it was because God was looking out for me. I had planned to push her off the ferry when no one was looking. You see, I was living in Staten Island, and I gave her one hundred dollars to go to Manhattan and buy drugs for me. Well, I waited and waited, and she never came back. You know what happened, right?"

"She shot the drugs she bought with your money."

"I can tell you've been around. Did that ever happen to you?"

"Twice. But I'll tell you, one of the worst problems is when you buy drugs from a pusher and it's nothing but garbage. Just plain white milk sugar, but no heroin. A couple of times I've felt like killing the pushers!"

"Well, anyway, there I was," Monique continued, "stomping up and down that ferry. Every time we docked at Manhattan, I'd go to the front and wait for her. She didn't show.

"As we headed back to Staten Island, I was at the rail—and I was burning. Then I got this overwhelming fear of jumping into those dark waters myself. I was miserable. I'd been an addict for six years and had gotten nowhere.''

Cindy could identify with that. It hadn't been too many days ago that she had taken that gun in her hand . . . . Had God really intervened to keep her from killing herself?

"As I was leaning against that rail, I noticed these two girls and a man next to me. The thing that struck me was that one of them talked as if she was from the South. You know, she had that funny accent.''

Cindy nodded. Southerners were easy to detect.

"I don't know why, but I was irritated by the way that girl was talking, so I blurted out, 'If I had known you were coming, I would have saved you the trip and sent you a postcard of the Statue of Liberty.' ''

"You said *that* to people you didn't know?''

"I know it was a smart-aleck remark. Right after I said it, I thought, *What a stupid thing to say!* They could have picked me up and thrown me into the river. But she just looked at me and smiled. I continued to stare at that dark water.

"Then she walked over ånd put her arm around my shoulders. I got real nervous. She didn't look like a lesbian or anything like that, so I wondered if she was trying to mug me. But I didn't have a purse.

"Out of the clear blue sky she said to me, 'Jesus loves you.'

"You can imagine how I felt. Here I was, out in the middle of the Hudson River, ready to kill a girl, and this strange-talking woman comes up, puts her arm around me, and tells me Jesus loves me. I almost flipped.

"And if that wasn't enough, she said she was from

the Walter Hoving Home, a home for girls like me. I wondered, *Does this girl know what I'm up to? How could she? Who told her?* I became very defensive and said, 'Like me?' "

Cindy leaned forward.

"Then I lied to her and said, 'What do you mean— like me? I'm no dirty, filthy junkie. I'm out here enjoying the good old scenery on this night.'

"But that wouldn't stop her. She said she had been working with addicts for many years and could tell one. Then she reached down and put her finger on my track. That really blew my cover."

Cindy laughed. There was no way to cover the track. And Monique had a big track.

"So I thought I might as well come clean with her. I told her about being on drugs for six years. She stood there, hanging on every word I said. I could feel the compassion flowing from her heart out to me."

Cindy knew about that compassion. Mrs. Redfield had it. The staff at the Home had it—and now Monique. Cindy wondered if all Christians had compassion.

Monique continued, "That staff worker, incidentally, was Frances Wingate. You met Frannie; she's the one in charge of the work program."

Frannie had become a special friend to Cindy. She also had been an addict. She really knew where it was at.

"Well, anyway, I told Frannie about having been in and out of mental institutions, going to psychiatrists, and trying various drug-rehabilitation programs. She really identified and began telling me about her past life. Then she told me how Christ had saved her and brought her to the Home. What a relief to find someone who had actually been helped!

"Frannie gave me the address of the Home and told me to call if I ever needed help. But you know how that is; I always needed help, but I didn't think I'd find it at the Walter Hoving Home.

"So I went home. Fortunately I didn't see the girl who had ripped me off. But when I got home, I just couldn't get away from Frannie's compassion. She seemed so confident that Christ could help me. Of course I had been in and out of many programs. You know, the only reason you go through a program is so you can just kind of lay up for a while and get clean so you can go out and get a quick high again.

"The next day when I got up, I decided I had nothing to lose, so I called the Home. Believe me, from the very first hello on the telephone until now I can honestly say that the staff have really committed their lives to helping me.

"I went up that day for an interview. You know, when you walk in the front room, you can really feel the warmth and love that seem to come out of the walls.

"In fact I'll have to tell you something funny. Mr. Hoving, the man the Home is named after, is the chairman of Tiffany's. A few years ago Reverend Benton, the director, had to give serious thought to selling the property because of zoning problems. When Reverend Benton told Mr. Hoving, he said, "You can't sell the Home. Jesus is in those walls up there!"

Cindy chuckled. Yes, Jesus was everywhere!

"When I walked in that door for my interview," Monique went on, "there was one great big problem. I was high."

"You were high?"

"Yes. I got scared about riding on the train. So I lied to my mother about the cost of the ticket and got an extra ten dollars from her. I used that to get off.

"Of course the people around here aren't stupid. They knew right away what was wrong, and they said I had to go home and wait a couple of days.

"I was mad, but I knew they were right. It wouldn't be good for me to be high around those girls who were trying to make it.

"So I went home and started to kick. I got restless and went out by the front fence. A taxi driver, an old friend of one of my 'johns,' came by and gave me the eye. I got in, and we went out by the seashore. He gave me twenty-five dollars. But would you believe that when I came back, I had no desire to get high? Those people up at the Home must have really been praying for me.

"But I did suffer some tragic consequences from my sin with that taxi driver. The guy had VD, and I got a bad case.

"Well, anyway, I went back to the Home. By this time I was really sick. They immediately put me to bed, and somebody prayed and stayed with me to check on how I was getting along.

"I finally got through the kicking and started with the classes. It was all so strange."

"I know how you felt," Cindy interrupted. "It's really different."

"But then a few days later I gave my life to Christ," Monique said. "I think the thing that really changed me was that I couldn't get over how Christ gave His life for me. He died that I might live. He was bound to the cross that I might be set free. Even to this day the thought of Jesus doing all this for me just overwhelms me.'' Monique wiped a tear from her eye. ''Think of it—He loved me enough to die for me!

''Cindy, I know it's not easy for you. It wasn't for me either. But you know something? If it had been easy all the way through, I don't think I would have grown spiritually. It seems to me that spiritual growth and difficulties go hand in hand. I've noticed that after I've gone through some hard places, it seems I've grown a foot taller in the Lord!''

Cindy knew Monique was telling her the truth. She bowed her head. Then looking back at Monique, she said, ''I don't know what lies ahead for me. But I really do believe God controls my future, and I want to follow Him.''

''That's right, Cindy. You're on the right track now. Just trust God. Would you mind if I prayed?''

''I would like that.''

Monique bowed her head. She prayed that the temptations of the world would leave Cindy alone and that she would stay and learn how to develop spiritual maturity. Monique's prayer touched Cindy. She wouldn't leave yet.

The next evening was Monday-night prayer time. Cindy felt an intense desire to really make things right with God. She knew that's what it would take for her to make it through. So over in a corner of the room, all by herself, she opened up to God. The tears flowed unhindered as she said, ''Lord Jesus, I need You. I open the door of my life and receive You as my Saviour and Lord. Thank You for forgiving my sins. Take control of the throne of my life. Make me the kind of person You want me to be.''

That was it: no bells, no fireworks. But, oh, what peace! What joy!

She leaned over and tapped Judy on the shoulder.

"Judy, I just had to tell you. Right now I gave my life over to Jesus!"

"Oh, Cindy I'm so happy for you!" Judy threw her arms around her. "You'll never regret it!"

In the days that followed, Cindy still had problems—as any young Christian has. But she was determined to stick with Jesus all the way. That determination brought new challenges; but through prayer, memorizing Scriptures and putting them into practice, and responding to God's way, Cindy was growing in the Lord.

They certainly did keep the girls busy at the Walter Hoving Home. During the morning Bible classes they learned what God's Word taught. Then there were the personal-improvement classes, work program, cooking, office work, yard and house maintenance, and all the rest—it certainly didn't leave much time for depression. And they also had shopping trips, choir performances, outings, and visits to senior citizens.

And there was always the horse, Sertsey, to ride. As a little girl Cindy had dreamed of being a cowgirl. That could never be, but it was so much fun to ride around the field on Sertsey, relaxing and thinking about the goodness of God.

During class one morning, Sally Bowers, the education director, told Cindy she had a telephone call from the Bureau of Child Welfare.

Had something happened to Melody?

With every hurried step from the Learning Center to the main house, Cindy tried to think of what she would do if Melody had died. She was met at the door by Mrs. Benton.

"Cindy, you look terrified. I'm not sure it's serious, so don't draw any conclusions."

That was so like Mrs. Benton—always encouraging and helping. She was the one who always gave you a big hug and kiss. She had been wonderful to Cindy.

In fact all the staff were wonderful, she reflected.

It was fun working in the office with Joyce Dyrud, the office manager. The others in the office—Mildred Rogers and Joyce's mom, Lillian—also possessed great patience. If you made a mistake, they never did come down hard. They would just repeat the instructions. They were real Christians!

She still remembered how Bev Zechar had stayed up with her one night when she was so terribly sick. Bev was always ready to help anyone in need. And the days spent in the Learning Center with Linda Wahl and Stephanie Haas were so helpful!

There was Papa Dyrud painting. She waved. What great patience he had with the girls in the yard crew.

And, of course, the Benton's children—Marji, Connie, Jim, and David—were always a lot of fun to be around.

Now she hurried into the office to pick up the phone. "Hello, this is Cindy."

"Cindy, this is Mrs. Shephard—you know, the lady you turned your child over to. I've been instructed by the court to call you and let you know Melody has been placed in temporary custody. Some people have expressed an intense desire to adopt her. We were wondering if we could talk to you about that."

"No! No! No!" Cindy screamed into the phone. "No one, and I mean *no one,* can adopt Melody! Do you understand what I'm saying, Mrs. Shephard?''

"Now, Cindy, calm down . . . ."

"If you think for one minute that you're going to take my daughter away from me permanently, you've had it! For all these months now I've wondered about her; I will not give her up! I want her back!''

The rush of words brought her to the point of tears.

"Please, Cindy, we're not here to take away your daughter. We were just trying to find out if you were interested. I must say, you've expressed yourself very clearly. I'll tell these people that Melody isn't available.''

Cindy drew a deep breath. That was close!

"And, Cindy, how are you doing there? I've read a few things about the Home and understand it's a very nice place.''

"Yes, Mrs. Shephard, it is. In fact it's a wonderful place. They really let Christ shine through their lives here.''

There was a long pause. Mrs. Shephard wasn't a Christian.

"I received Jesus Christ as my personal Saviour; and as I study His Word about how to respond to life, He is really doing some great things for me. I've experienced the miracle of being born again.''

Another long pause.

"I hope someday to see you in person and tell you of the great change that has taken place in my life.''

Still another long pause. Something was wrong! Suddenly Cindy knew what it was—the way she had responded to Mrs. Shephard. That wasn't the way she had been taught to respond. When confronting a crisis, one should respond in love.

Cindy then did what she had been taught to do when she had responded wrongly. "Mrs. Shephard, will you forgive me for the way I answered when you called about Melody? You see, I really had given her over to the Lord. It looks as though I grabbed her back out of His arms. Would you please forgive me for my wrong attitude?"

There was yet another long pause.

"Mrs. Shephard, are you still there?"

"Yes, Cindy. I've never really had something like this happen to me in all the years I've been a social worker. I've faced all kinds of people with all kinds of tempers. Once a mother drew a gun on me, and I thought I had had it. But never before has someone asked me to forgive them.

"Of course I'll forgive you. And I'll stay in touch with you. Someday maybe I can visit you at the Home. It must be one place in a thousand. I know a few other girls who could really benefit from the help you're getting."

"Oh, please come! I'd just love for you to see the Home!"

Cindy stepped more lightly as she walked back to the Learning Center. She kept going back over the conversation. She was so thankful that Melody wasn't being sent to someone else.

Then she realized she had forgotten to ask how Melody was getting along. Evidently she must have been all right.

Cindy knew she had learned an important lesson. She'd learned how to ask people to forgive her when she made mistakes. Yes, God was giving her opportunities to grow!

9

Winter had come to the Walter Hoving Home. Cindy never had liked winter in the city. There the snow was always gray. Here in Garrison it was a beautiful white. It was so invigorating, so clean.

She soon adjusted to walking on slippery snow and bundling up her coat extra tight to keep out the cold. And life went on regardless of how much it snowed.

About eight one evening she was called to the phone. Who could it be? Certainly she didn't have many friends, at least not yet.

"Hello, this is Cindy."

"Cindy, my darling, this is your mother. How are you doing?"

Cindy couldn't believe it. It had been almost three years since she had heard from her mother. She did write home to let them know she was at the Walter Hoving Home but had never heard from her parents. She figured they had written her off.

"Oh, Mother, it's so good to hear your voice. How have you been?"

"Just fine, darling. Of course I've been wondering how you've been doing. I didn't call sooner because I was afraid it might upset you, and you'd go back out in the streets and return to your drugs. So your father and I thought we should just wait. Now we felt it was the time to call. And you say you're doing all right?"

"Yes, Mother, I have been doing the best I ever have done in my whole life. Jesus is so wonderful to me. I just can't love Him enough for changing my life. I just wish I had known Him since I was a child."

"Don't tell me you've become a Jesus freak?"

Cindy laughed. "No, Mother. I've just become a born-again Christian! That's all!"

"Well, you scared me half to death. I thought the next thing you'd be doing was packing a sleeping bag and going off in the woods and staring up at the sun to get revelations. I've heard about those kids doing that, and all they end up with is blindness. Some of them even freeze to death."

Cindy chuckled again. That was just like her mother. Always exaggerating and getting alarmed about anything out of the ordinary.

"Mother, why don't you and Daddy come up and visit me?" Cindy said. "I know you'd just love this place the Lord has given us. Most of all, I'd like you to meet the other girls and the staff here at the Home. I know you'd really feel love here like no other place you've ever been. Maybe it will help you understand what I'm talking about."

"Thank you, Cindy. I'm sure it would be wonderful. But your father and I haven't been getting along too well lately. He just won't stop drinking, and he's gotten very sick. I really think that if he doesn't stop, it won't be much longer until he's dead!"

The silence gave Cindy time to remember that her father had had this drinking problem for years now. This is what it led to. She had heard that alcoholism was killing more people than wars. Would her father be the next victim?

"Well, Mom, tell Daddy there is really hope for him too. You know how I struggled for years with drugs, and Christ set me free. I know He wants to do the same for Daddy with alcohol. Do you think he can come?"

"No, honey, I don't think so. I can hardly get him out of the house. About all I can do is get him into the car and off to work. His job occupies him enough, but I'm afraid of his driving at times. He's worked at the same place now for twenty-five years, and I don't think they would fire him. I secretly fear they know it's almost the end for him. Goodness knows what I'll do if he dies."

"Mama, why don't you ask Daddy again if he could come up with you. Tomorrow is Sunday, and some of the girls have visitors in the afternoon. It would be so nice if you and Daddy could come. With the snow on the ground and these beautiful trees, it's just like a picture postcard here. Could you come? Please?"

"I'll try, honey—one way or the other. If we can't come, I'll call. But if we can, we'll be there about two."

Cindy could hardly sleep that night. It would be so good to see her parents again.

Cindy found it hard to keep her mind on the chapel service on Sunday morning. She picked at her food at lunch, so anxious was she about seeing her mother and dad.

It started to snow again. The weather report didn't sound encouraging, and she became concerned. But her mother would be driving, and she was careful.

A little past two Cindy was staring out the dining-room window. Through the snow she could just make out a car. She strained to see. There was just one person in it. Then she recognized her mother and began jumping up and down like a schoolgirl.

Not worrying about throwing on her coat, Cindy

dashed out the front door. As soon as her mother got out of the car, Cindy was there, throwing her arms around her and crying. "Oh, Mother, it's so good to see you. It seems like it's been twenty years. I've longed so much to feel your arms around me."

"Cindy, darling, I feel the same about you. Even the time you came home to kick your habit, I tried to put my arms around you, but you pushed them away. You didn't want our help then. But it's so different now!"

Mrs. Lippincot began to cry too. They stayed there in each other's arms, laughing and crying. It was the way God had intended it to be—a mother who can comfort her daughter.

"Come on, Mom. Let's go inside before we freeze!"

Once inside, Cindy excitedly introduced her mother to some of the other girls. Then she spied Mrs. Benton. "Mrs. Benton, this is my mother, Gloria Lippincot. Mother, this is Mrs. Benton, the wife of our director."

"Welcome, Mrs. Lippincot. We're so happy you could come. We're proud of the progress Cindy is making. Christ has done something very real in her heart. Now we want her to be reunited with you and her father—once again to be part of her family. When God created us, He really created us as families. Sin and drug addiction have torn your family apart. But God wants to reestablish it with love."

"And, Mom," Cindy added, "I really believe that God is going to do something special for you and Daddy."

"Well, I certainly hope so. I'm really at the end of myself trying to figure out your father. If something doesn't happen soon, I think I'm going to crack up."

Mrs. Lippincot stared at the floor. Tears welled in her eyes and rolled down her cheeks. Mrs. Benton reached over and hugged her. "Mrs. Lippincot," she said, "that's where Christ really wants to come into your life: at the end of your rope—that's where Jesus always is."

"I must confess I really don't understand all that has happened to Cindy," Mrs. Lippincot said as she regained her composure. "All this God bit. I thought I was a good person, but something dramatic has certainly happened to Cindy. I'm not a drug addict or anything like that, but I do wish something could happen to me!"

"Mom, that's what I was trying to tell you on the phone last night. Jesus wants to make a difference in all our lives."

"Well, honey, after I finished talking to you, I went to Daddy and asked if he would come up here with me today. He got very upset and started cursing. He said that you were wrecking his life. He blamed his drinking on you, Cindy. Then he said he wouldn't have anything more to do with you because of all the heartache you caused him."

Cindy blinked back her tears as she looked questioningly at Mrs. Benton.

"It's not uncommon for parents to respond that way, Mrs. Lippincot. I know Cindy is much different than she used to be, but sometimes it is very difficult to convince parents that something real is happening."

"Even when I wanted to come up here, my husband almost refused," Mrs. Lippincot said. "We argued, and he finally consented. He did tell me to drive carefully, so I guess he does care about me—at least a little. I'm sorry for the way he feels about you, Cindy."

"Mom, don't worry about that. You really can't

blame Daddy. You know how I was. I *did* cause you both a lot of heartaches. I really didn't want to be a drug addict, but it happened, and I had to live with that curse.

"Oh, how I wish I could just roll back the years and be to you and Daddy the daughter that God intended me to be. God has showed me so many things I missed because I missed His will for my life.

"You know what I really want, Mama? I want to come back home and love you and Daddy the way I should. I want to be that obedient daughter and make life a blessing instead of a curse for you and Daddy. I know I could never undo all the trouble I gave you. I'll just have to trust the Lord to help me be a blessing to you from now on."

Mrs. Lippincot reached over and hugged her daughter again. "I never thought I'd hear you say things like that, Cindy. I just wish I had what you have. It sure takes an awful lot even to try to love your father. His drinking has made life unbearable. I don't know the answer."

"I know the answer," Mrs. Benton said softly.

"Sure, I know the answer too. Hit Harvey over the head and send him to his grave!"

"Mom, don't say things like that!"

"Well, I guess I'm just kidding. But there certainly is no answer to my problem."

"Yes, there is," Mrs. Benton persisted. "Do you want me to tell you the answer?"

"Mrs. Benton, if you tell me the answer, you'll be my friend forever!"

"Well, it's very simple. Why don't you let Jesus come into your life and begin to work out all these problems for you? I'm not saying that if you turn your life over to Jesus, your husband will have a turn-around, but what I am saying is this: When you receive Jesus as your personal Saviour, He has something available to help you go through any trial and still make it."

Gloria Lippincot looked at her. "Do you really believe what you're telling me?"

"Of course I do. I've seen the Lord work absolute miracles. Take one of our girls, Winnie. She went through the program with a jail sentence hanging over her head. To make a long story short, when she completed our program, she landed back in a federal penitentiary in Pennsylvania. Can you imagine this beautiful young lady having to go back to the hell of a prison? Well, she did. But while she was there, she remained a wonderful Christian. She found the secret I'm telling you about. She found that God gave her grace in prison.

"I'm not saying you have to go to prison. But when you go back home into the hell you face there, God can give you the grace to look objectively at your husband. You won't see him as an alcoholic, but as a person who needs to know Jesus' love too. And that all starts from coming to know Jesus as your Saviour."

"You make it sound so simple, Mrs. Benton. But does it really work?"

"Well, there's one way to find out. One verse in the Bible encourages us to 'taste and see that the Lord is good.' You know what that means: If you don't take a bite of something, you'll never know how it tastes. God wants you to try Him."

"How does this happen?" Mrs. Lippincot asked.

Mrs. Benton and Cindy smiled at each other.

"Why don't the three of us go down to the prayer

room, and I'll explain from the Bible how all this happens. Okay?''

Cindy knew Mrs. Benton had taken many people to that prayer room. This was the place where many parents had come to know Jesus as their Saviour. She had also prayed with others to receive the baptism of the Holy Spirit to give them greater spiritual power in living the Christian life.

In a few minutes Mrs. Lippincot was repeating the ''sinner's prayer'' and receiving Jesus as her personal Saviour. It seemed so natural, so wonderful, and so easy and powerful!

Cindy said she felt like jumping up and down again: she was so happy.

They knew Gloria Lippincot's new experience would be severely tested when she got back home, so they spent time helping her develop a pattern for her Christian life. Cindy knew God's grace had sustained her; it would work for her mother too!

Mrs. Benton excused herself to attend to some other matters, and Cindy and her mother got in some real mother-daughter talk the rest of the afternoon. It was just starting to get dark when Mrs. Lippincot said she really had to leave; her husband would worry if she were too late.

As they walked toward the car, Cindy said, ''I really love you, Mother. It's so wonderful to know that you and I are now Christians. We're really members of the family of God. Tonight I'm really going to pray that Daddy will get saved too.''

''Thank you, honey. I'm so happy. I know something has happened on the inside of me. When I go back home, I'm going to ask God to give me that grace Mrs. Benton talked about. I want to be the wife God intended me to be, the same way you said you wanted to be the daughter God wanted you to be, and I've got a sneaking suspicion it's going to work!''

They were at the car now, and Cindy was helping brush away the new snow. "Mom, please come back whenever you can. You're always welcome to visit here. Brother Benton said this place doesn't belong to him and the staff; it belongs to God. So he wants to share God's blessings with everyone. Makes you feel good when a person has that attitude—right?''

"Right! Maybe that's why someone like me can feel the presence of the Lord here at the Home. This surely is God's house!''

Cindy hugged and kissed her mother again. It seemed so right.

It was still snowing lightly as Gloria Lippincot drove away. *I forgot to tell her to drive carefully,* Cindy thought as she started back to the house. She knew the roads would be slippery, and she wanted to be sure her mother arrived home safely to bring the message of hope and peace to her father. Maybe he would listen to her. Maybe he too would receive Jesus as his Saviour. And if that happened, would he be more ready to let her come home?

The snow increased in intensity that night, so Brother Benton decided not to take the girls out to church, as they usually did on Sunday night. Instead they made a roaring fire in the living-room fireplace and had chapel in front of it. It was so cozy and so nice. And Cindy was so happy that she could hardly contain her joy.

The girls usually got to sleep in on Monday. Quite often the choir had ministry somewhere on Sunday night, and they got home late, so the girls were allowed some rest and relaxation on Monday morning.

But at 7:30 that Monday morning Mrs. Benton entered Cindy's room and gently called her.

Cindy woke with a start. What was Mrs. Benton doing here? What day was it? Cindy couldn't quite get her thoughts together.

"What's the matter? Did I oversleep?"

"No, you didn't oversleep. It's Monday. I've made some fresh coffee. Would you like some?"

"Sounds great, Mrs. Benton. Do you always bring coffee to the girls on Monday morning?"

"Not usually. Why don't you slip your bathrobe on, and let's go downstairs and have a cup together. Okay?"

Why would Mrs. Benton come up and invite me to have coffee with her? Cindy wondered as she ran a brush through her hair. *Was something the matter?*

In the kitchen Mrs. Benton poured the coffee. "Let's take it into my little office," she suggested.

"Is something the matter?" Cindy asked. "Am I going to be dismissed?"

"No, Cindy. Girls are dismissed from here only because something drastic has gone wrong."

They walked into the office. Mrs. Benton closed the door, motioning for Cindy to sit in the chair next to the desk.

"Cindy, I have something to tell you, and I didn't want to tell you in your bedroom. I felt we should talk here."

"Something's happened to Melody!" Cindy wailed.

"No, not as far as I know. But something very serious has happened to your mother."

"Mother? Did Daddy beat her up when she got

home? What happened?'' Cindy was on the edge of her chair, the coffee forgotten.

''I am very sorry to tell you this, but your mother has passed away.''

''Passed away!'' Cindy screamed. ''Oh, my God. What am I going to do now? My mother is dead!''

Cindy began shaking violently, and Mrs. Benton reached over to comfort her. She put her cheek against Cindy's and held her tight. The tears flowed freely.

Neither spoke. What can you say to a person who has just lost her mother?

Finally through her sobs Cindy choked out the words, ''How did it happen? Was she in an accident . . . or what?''

''The roads were very slippery last night,'' Mrs. Benton answered. ''Your mother apparently was doing all right, but a truck coming toward her lost control, slid over, and hit your mother's car head on. The state patrol said she was killed instantly.''

''I just can't believe it,'' Cindy sobbed. ''Just here last night I held my mother in my arms and kissed her good-bye. Now she's dead!''

''The patrol came a little while ago, dear. I thought maybe they were bringing a runaway or a hitchhiker who needed a place to stay. But when I met the officer at the door, he told me the news. He wanted to know whether or not it would be better if I told you, and I said I thought it might be. Your father has been contacted. In fact I understand he told the state patrol about your being up here.''

Cindy just couldn't stop crying. It had seemed as though everything was coming along just fine. She had found out she might get Melody back. Then her mother got saved. The future looked so bright—now this.

"Mrs. Benton, why did my mother die?"

"Honey, I guess that's a question almost everyone asks when someone dear to them dies. And we really can't answer it. We have to leave it in God's hands.

"When Brother Benton and I were missionaries in Japan, I gave birth to a beautiful red-haired boy. Two days later he was dead. We don't know why he died.

"I suppose it was harder for Brother Benton than for me. You see, he had to sell everything we had for us to get to Japan as missionaries. I was expecting when we got there, and he'd always wanted to have a red-haired boy. We had our oldest daughter Marji by then, and this beautiful little boy was born to us. We named him Jerry.

"But two days later he passed away. It was as though our world had stopped.

"Brother Benton had to make all the arrangements for the funeral. He even had to carry a shovel at the funeral to bury our little boy's body.

"It was very hard for us after the funeral. Especially for Brother Benton. He couldn't understand after all he had done, why God would take his little son away from him.

"In those dark days we really had no one to turn to. We were strangers in a foreign country."

Mrs. Benton paused to dry a tear.

"Then a few weeks after this God showed Brother Benton a verse in the Bible where God talks about how he should continue his ministry with joy. I don't know exactly what happened, but something did when he read that Bible verse. God spoke to us. We reached out for His grace. And He brought us back up again.

"Now, Cindy, to this day we don't know why our son Jerry died. But I'll tell you one thing. God's grace sustained us through those days of trying to get back on top. We made it through. God knows best."

Cindy was still trying to dry her tears. "I really don't know what to do next. I suppose I should contact my father."

"Yes, but before that, I want to have prayer with you. Just think, Cindy. We can thank God that your mother received Jesus as her personal Saviour before she died. She's at home now with the Lord. And someday you'll be reunited with her in heaven. We have that great hope that to be absent from the body is to be present with the Lord."

Mrs. Benton began to ask for God's special grace for Cindy. As she prayed, Cindy began to experience an inexplicable peace, a confidence she would see her mother again. Then they both prayed for Cindy's father.

When Mrs. Benton reached Mr. Lippincot on the phone, she said, "I'm so sorry about your wife. We just got the word. This is Mrs. Benton from the Walter Hoving Home where Cindy is. She's in the office with me now. We've just had a word of prayer together, and we asked God to give His grace to Cindy and you at this trying time."

Mr. Lippincot didn't say a word.

"Would you like to speak to Cindy?"

Another long pause. Then, "Mrs. Benton, I don't ever want to speak to Cindy again. If Gloria hadn't listened to her and driven up there yesterday, she'd still be living. It's Cindy's fault that my wife is dead!"

There was a click. He had hung up!

10

The next day Mrs. Benton saw Cindy right after breakfast and took her back to the little office to talk some more—this time without coffee.

"Cindy, I think we should try to call your father once again," she said. "I'm sure he has thought through what has happened. Maybe this morning he's a little better. You know, it's quite a shock to lose a loved one. So let's hope and pray he will be more responsive. And I know you want to attend the funeral. We need to find out about that."

Mrs. Benton dialed. After exchanging greetings, she handed the telephone to Cindy.

"Daddy, this is Cindy. How are you doing?"

"About as well as can be expected."

"Daddy, I just wanted to tell you once again how sorry I am that Mother passed away."

"I'm sorry too—very sorry. It's just too bad that you had to come into our lives. You're the one who caused all this."

Cindy remained silent. Obviously her father still was not about to forgive her.

"Here I am left all alone in this world," he continued. "No one cares about me. You're supposed to be up there in that goody-goody home trying to get your life together. And here am I, left to myself with no one to care for me. I just knew your mother shouldn't have driven up to see you. I tried to tell her that the roads were bad. But she insisted because you wanted her to come. If it wasn't for you and all your trouble, she'd still be alive today and looking out for me."

"Daddy, please! I've told you I'm sorry for what happened. I'm sorry for the years of heartache I caused you and Mom. Don't you know that this hurts me as much as it hurts you? Just before Mom left here, I felt for the first time in my life I had finally found a mother. We hugged each other and kissed each other, and I felt warm love that I never felt before. Are you trying to tell me that what has happened doesn't hurt me? It cuts me clear to the heart!"

Mrs. Benton sat there quietly. She was pleased at the maturity Cindy was showing. But she knew there would be further problems between Cindy and her father.

"And, Daddy, let me tell you one more thing. You and I have a wonderful hope. Mother is at peace with the Lord. While she was up here on Sunday, she was born again. So I know she's in heaven experiencing great joy. Did you know that?"

Mr. Lippincot didn't respond.

"Daddy, if you don't mind, I really would like to attend the funeral with you. I know I don't deserve a precious moment of being with you. I don't blame you for how you feel toward me. But would you please forgive me and let me attend the funeral?"

"Cindy, you can certainly attend her funeral. She was your mother as well as my wife, and I'll allow you that privilege. But I'll never forgive you for what you have done!"

Click went the receiver.

"What did he say, Cindy?"

"Well, Mrs. Benton, it wasn't good at all. He's still very bitter, but he did say I could attend the funeral. And he said he will never, never forgive me. Oh, what am I going to do to make him see that I've changed?"

"You must try to understand your father's position," Mrs. Benton answered. "With his enormous problem of alcoholism, these things can be very hard to take. He's all alone. But this is a wonderful opportunity for you to show him Christ's love. Let's pray right now for him. Prayer can change situations. God can show you how to give your father that love you have experienced."

Mom Benton reached over and put her hand on Cindy's shoulder. Once again Cindy felt that calming, that peace as they prayed.

The Bentons took Cindy to the funeral. A few neighbors and some friends from Mr. Lippincot's work came. That was all.

At the close of the committal service at the cemetery, Pastor Schwartz asked Reverend Benton to pray. It was a prayer of hope and faith that someday Jesus would come back and that the Christians who are still alive will be caught up together with those who have gone on before.

As Cindy stood by the open grave, she knew that someday she would see her mother again, that they would both be forever with the Lord. Her tears were a montage of sorrow and joy—sorrow at the earthly parting, joy at the heavenly gain. If only her father could understand this!

Cindy went back to the Home after the funeral. But the horrible thought of her father being alone nagged her. She knew he blamed her for that aloneness.

So one evening she called him. He was drunk and hard to understand. But he said he was terribly sick and felt he was going to die. His bitterness toward her seemed to have subsided.

Cindy talked to Mrs. Benton and Shirley Swarthout about going home temporarily to help her father. They were both concerned. Could she stay true to the Lord under such trying circumstances? Would the pressure drive her back to drugs? Or had she developed the spiritual maturity she needed to handle the situation? Because of their uncertainty, they decided it would be best for her to go home for just a few days to see how it worked out. They would keep in close touch.

The next day when Cindy walked into her home, her father was lying on the couch. Next to him lay an empty bottle. He was asleep—dead drunk.

Everything was in total disarray, so Cindy decided to start by cleaning the house: washing, doing dishes, dusting, vacuuming. She half smiled when she remembered that not long ago she was content to live in far worse surroundings without trying to do anything about them!

Cindy had been working for about four hours when her father got up very slowly and sat on the edge of the couch.

"Cindy! What are you doing here?" he yelled.

"Daddy, I've come home to take care of you. Don't you remember? We talked about it on the phone last night."

"Talked? I don't remember talking to anyone last night. Why did you come? To torment me? Why don't you just head back to that Jesus place? I don't need your help!''

"Now just calm down, Daddy. When I talked to you last night, I knew you had been drinking. You probably don't remember it. So why don't you just lie back down and be quiet. I'm cleaning the house, and I'll fix you something to eat.''

Mr. Lippincot reached up and grabbed his forehead. "Oh, my head hurts," he moaned. "Whatever you do, do it quietly. My head feels like it's going to burst!'' With that he just sort of toppled back down again.

Cindy wondered what she could do to help her father, to show him she really loved him. His whiskey bottle was empty, and he would probably want another drink, but she decided that wouldn't be the thing to do. She noticed how bad he looked; his face was swollen.

"Poor thing!" she said to herself. "He probably hasn't eaten anything since Mom died.''

Then she remembered how he used to brag when she cooked beef Stroganoff. She decided to surprise him.

Of course the refrigerator was empty. So she walked to the store, bought what she needed, and hurried home to prepare it.

It smelled so good as it cooked. Every once in a while she tasted it. Excellent—the best she had ever fixed!

She found a tablecloth and set the table with her mother's good china and silverware. Then she walked into the living room and gently woke her father. "Daddy, it's time to eat. I've fixed something special for you!''

He sat up slowly. "What stinks around here? I smell something that stinks really horribly!''

Cindy laughed. "That's my cooking. I've made some of your favorite—beef Stróganoff!"

"Beef Stroganoff!" he yelled. "I don't want *anything* to eat, much less beef Stroganoff. Why don't you put it in the garbage can? From the smell, I'd say that's where it belongs!"

Cindy was crushed. She headed back into the kitchen, wondering how she could ever get through to her father. Obviously not through food!

Cindy knew she needed to eat something, but she just picked at the Stroganoff. How could she eat when her father had been so hateful?

After she had cleaned up the kitchen, she walked into the living room and turned on the TV.

"Shut that thing off! Can't you see I've got a headache?" Mr. Lippincot yelled.

He didn't have to tell Cindy twice to turn it off. Then she walked over to where he was. For the first time she really looked at him. He didn't have any shoes or socks on, and his feet were so swollen that it looked as if he had no ankles at all! His skin was yellow.

"Daddy, take a look at your feet and your coloring. Are you sure you're all right?"

"No, I'm not all right. I told you I'm sick. I can't even go to the bathroom. Something's wrong with me. I think I'm going to die!"

"Don't you think I should take you to the hospital?" Cindy expected another explosion. He never could stand the idea of being in a hospital.

"Maybe you should take me," he said rather meekly.

That really frightened Cindy. She threw her coat over her shoulders and rushed over to the Albert's.

They both came back with her.

One look was enough for Mr. Albert. He quickly brought his car around to the front. The three of them carried her father to the car and got him into the backseat. They rushed him to the emergency room, where some doctors examined him and took him upstairs.

One of the doctors called Cindy into his office.

"I understand you're the daughter of Harvey Lippincot?" he asked.

"Yes, sir."

"Your neighbors told me about your mother's being killed in an accident. So all you have left is your father?"

"That's right."

"Well, I have some very serious news, Cindy. Your father is suffering from acute alcoholism. His body is so swollen that some of his vital organs aren't functioning well. Unless something unusual happens, your father has only a couple of weeks to live. I'm sorry."

"A couple of weeks?" Cindy said. "Oh, no!" She couldn't believe what she was hearing.

The doctor was continuing in his professional way, "Of course we will do the best we can. We've seen some people make a complete turnabout. We will do everything medically possible for your father. But it just doesn't look good."

"Thank you, doctor. I'll try to do the best I can."

"Do you have a place to stay or someone to stay with you?"

"Not really. I've been up at Garrison, New York, at the Walter Hoving Home. I'm a former drug addict. When my mother passed away, I came home to take care of my father. I know they would want me to go back.''

''I think that would be best,'' the doctor said. ''A home can be awfully empty with only one person living in it.''

Cindy was quite discouraged when she arrived back at the Walter Hoving Home. But the girls there had been having special prayer for her. Just knowing they were concerned helped lift her spirits.

The following day Mrs. Benton took Cindy back to visit Mr. Lippincot. He lay very still, needles and tubes all over him.

''Daddy, it's Cindy.''

Harvey Lippincot opened his eyes with great difficulty. He slowly reached over and touched Cindy's hand. Then he took hold of it and squeezed it slightly. ''Cindy, I'm very sick. I really don't know if I'm going to make it. I've lived such a miserable life. I couldn't sleep at all last night, and I got to thinking about the mess I've made of my life. I haven't been the father to you that I should have been. I just wish I'd have another chance. But I think it's too late.''

Cindy's eyes brimmed with tears. Her father started to cry too.

Mrs. Benton reached over and put an arm around Cindy and placed the other on Mr. Lippincot's shoulder.

''All of us at the Home have grieved with you in the enormous problems you have faced these last few days, sir. We too have wept at the loss of your wife. But a wonderful thing happened to her before she died. She accepted Jesus and received eternal life from Him. Now she's with Him!

"Did you know she's in heaven waiting for the day she can be reunited with you and Cindy? Have you ever thought of giving your life over to Jesus and receiving eternal life?"

"No, Mrs. Benton, I guess I haven't. A couple of times Gloria watched Rex Humbard and Oral Roberts on TV—even Billy Graham. Something deep inside wanted me to say yes to receiving Christ, but I just passed it over."

"Many people are like that," Mrs. Benton said. "They don't think it's very serious. But it is! And I want to be honest with you, Mr. Lippincot. This may be the only chance you'll ever have to receive Jesus as your Saviour. Receive Him now. Don't miss this greatest opportunity of your life!"

"Daddy, why don't you let me pray with you to receive Jesus as your Saviour? It's not hard. It just takes your will. If you'll submit your will to the Lord and ask Him to forgive all your sins and invite Him into your heart, Jesus comes, and He brings eternal life. That means you'll live forever! Maybe not on this earth, but in heaven. Would you like to receive Jesus as your Saviour?"

Harvey Lippincot turned his face toward the wall. The silence seemed like an eternity.

Then he turned back toward Cindy. "Yes, I do, " he said. "I want to receive Jesus."

Cindy then led her father in the "sinner's prayer."

"Now, Dad, you've been born again. Jesus has come into your life, and you are saved."

"I feel so clean!" Mr. Lippincot exalted. "I'm so happy! I'm going to be like you and live for Jesus the rest of my life!"

"Cindy," Mrs. Benton said, "do you realize what's happened? You just led your first person to the Lord!"

The three of them chuckled together.

"Dad, I'll come to see you every day. Believe me, all of us at the Home are going to continue to pray for you."

Just before she left, Cindy reached down and kissed her father's cheek.

"Cindy, honey, lean down here again, please."

When she did, he reached out as best he could and put his arms around her, drawing her close to himself. Then he kissed her cheek. Cindy started to cry again.

"Cindy, for the first time in my life I feel like a real father. Oh, I wish I hadn't waited so long . . . ."

Cindy stood there a moment. She looked at his body wracked with pain and disease. But his spirit was alive and well; that was showing in his face! What a miracle!

The next day Cindy went to visit him again. What a wonderful time they had as they talked about the Lord and the many promises in His Word about the future. Mr. Lippincot kept talking about heaven and seeing his wife again.

Cindy visited him every day. Then at four one morning the final call came.

Mrs. Benton had come to Cindy's room. As soon as she awakened, Cindy knew what had happened. "Dad has passed on, hasn't he?"

"Yes, the hospital just called. They said he died in his sleep. The nurse told me she just couldn't get over the tremendous change that came over him since he became a Christian."

"Just think, Mrs. Benton. Now Dad is with Mom. He won't have any more pain or sorrow or tears. I just can't believe the Lord would do all these wonderful things for me."

"Yes," Mrs. Benton agreed, "the Lord has indeed prepared a wonderful future for us—both in this life and in heaven!"

Cindy got out of bed and slipped into her bathrobe. Strange! She felt a great sense of relief. Of course she would miss her mother and father deeply. Especially since she had just come into this new life in Christ. But how satisfying it was to know that both of them were in heaven. And her dad was over his suffering.

That afternoon Cindy made the funeral arrangements. She asked Reverend Benton to conduct it.

Frannie, one of the staff members, never called a Christian's funeral a "funeral." She said it was celebrating a "home-going."

All the girls and staff were invited to Mr. Lippincot's "home-going." It provided a wonderful opportunity to testify to visitors of the hope all Christians have. The hope of eternal life.

Once again Cindy stood by an open grave. This time it was next to her mother's. She knew it was just a temporary separation. Her real father wasn't going into the ground. He had already gone to heaven!

The rest of the year went quickly for Cindy as she completed the program at the Walter Hoving Home. When graduation finally came, she was so excited. She had been accepted by Southeastern College in Lakeland, Florida. And she had an offer to work at a Christian delinquent girls' home while attending college. She would be a part-time counselor.

Graduation was beautiful! She was rewarded for her faithfulness to God and to His Word for that completed year.

The day after graduation she headed back to the city. Not to get high, though! She had an appointment to see Mrs. Shephard about her daughter.

She was nervous. Would Melody accept her as a mother?

The elevator to Mrs. Shephard's office brought back some painful memories. She hesitatingly opened the door to Mrs. Shephard's office. Sitting on a chair in a darling little pink dress was Melody. How she had grown!

As soon as Melody spied her mother she flew out of the chair. "Mommy! Mommy! Mommy! I love you! I love you!"

The two threw their arms around each other, hugging and kissing as if they would never stop.

"My little darling, you look so good!"

Mrs. Shephard walked over. "My! This is a glad reunion!" she said.

"Cindy, we've been keeping track of your progress at the Home. They told me about the tragic deaths of your mother and father. But I'm told you adjusted very well."

"Thank you, Mrs. Shephard. And by the looks of Melody, she's been very well taken care of. I want to thank you for that."

"I have some good news, Cindy. The court has decided it would be best to return Melody to you. Do you want her?"

"Want her? Having Melody would be the most wonderful thing that could ever happen to me!

When can I have her?"

"When can you have her?" Mrs. Shephard smiled. "You already have her. She's yours!"

Cindy squealed with joy. Then she reached down and threw her arms around Melody, picked her up, and squeezed her as hard as she could. Melody hugged back. It all seemed like a dream.

"Thank you, thank you, thank you, Mrs. Shephard. The Lord has been so good to me. Because of my drug addiction I almost lost everything in life. And now God has been so good in giving me back my Melody! Thank you so much!"

"You don't have to thank me, Cindy. Mrs. Benton and some of the counselors I've talked to kept telling me what you're saying. I clearly remember one of them expressing it, 'Jesus makes it all possible!' "

"That's it exactly," Cindy responded. "Jesus *does* make it all possible."

Cindy was still holding Melody when she walked out into the hallway. How different from the last time she was here! Then she ran to get away. Now she didn't want to let go, although Melody was getting heavy to carry!

When they got out on the street, Cindy finally put her down. Even a few New Yorkers were turning to look!

As the two walked hand in hand down Madison Avenue, Cindy kept remembering all the good things God had done for her. He had saved her, filled her with His Holy Spirit, and even given back her little daughter.

It was Madison Avenue, but it felt like heaven as she and Melody walked into their new life—together. .

Some good things are happening at The Walter Hoving Home.

Dramatic and beautiful changes have been taking place in the lives of many girls since the Home began in 1967. Ninety-four percent of the graduates who have come with problems such as narcotic addiction, alcoholism and delinquency have found release and happiness in a new way of living—with Christ. The continued success of this work is made possible through contributions from individuals who are concerned about helping a girl gain freedom from enslaving habits. Will you join with us in this work by sending a check?

The Walter Hoving Home
Box 194
Garrison, New York 10524
(914) 424-3674

Your Gifts Are Tax Deductible

The Walter Hoving Home.